Observations *of* Truth

OBSERVATIONS
of
TRUTH

JAMES BANDY

Epigraph Books
Rhinebeck, New York

Book and cover design by Georgia Dent

Library of Congress Control Number: 2010934490

ISBN: 978-0-9826441-8-8

Epigraph Books
27 Lamoree Road
Rhinebeck, New York 12572
www.epigraphPS.com
USA 845-876-4861

This is for my wife, the woman who showed me the truth that lies within us is real. She deserves everything this document can provide.

I love you.

FOREWORD

F OR THE PAST THIRTY YEARS I have been listening to people
talk about their lives. As a trained psychiatrist listening is a
skill that must be cultivated over time so that hearing your
patients is truly accomplished during the treatment process. In that
listening process people speak their truths, or more accurately, their
perception of their truths.

I was therefore curious when I was given the opportunity to
read James Bandy's 'Observations of Truth.' His book is a fascinat-
ing account of one mans journey into the nature of what is and the
power of inquiry through the nature of proof.

Bandy provides a clear, concise, easily understandable explanation of the role of causality and its application in achieving happiness.
This book demonstrates a reality based perspective that is meaningful
in elevating consciousness about making life choices.

Lewis S. Lane MD

Do not skip forward to a subject that interests you. That is not how this book is designed. One idea depends on an understanding from another idea. This book taken in content is important.

TABLE OF CONTENTS

INTRODUCTION

Because this book is based on observations of truth, I wish you to know me as I was, as I am and as I am trying to be.

I am what is generally considered a normal American male, raised in a middle-class family, without any religious traditions. I had little parental guidance after the age of eleven, although I was well taken care of and provided with much more than just the basic necessities of life by my family and friends, and I am still well cared for today.

My parents split up when I was eleven years old, an event that shocked my brother and me and most of their friends and family as well, because they appeared to be typically happy baby boomer parents. My father went to work each day and my mother took care of us kids and the home. Hardly ever did they argue. I have come to realize this was because they rarely communicated, beyond the basics of day-to-day life. The lack of communication and confrontation hid the growing dissatisfaction they held inside and ignored. As I've grown up and grown older, I've discovered this lack of communication is a common issue in many failed relationships.

With one parent absent and the other dealing with providing for her family, my brother and I had little supervision throughout our teenage years. Fortunately, I had enough sense to have some control over my behavior, but I had my share of stumbles along the way. Still, I was an easy teenager to deal with and was polite. I spent my time in the company of anyone who would accept me, but I never had any really close friends or relationships until after I graduated grade school.

Although I didn't realize it at the time, I feared almost everything in life, not knowing this was normal, for me and most other people. I found it hard to relate to others. I wanted to be more popular, accepted, but my inability to relate or become involved in conversations left little hope of accomplishing this. I had no idea why these desires felt so elusive.

Throughout my childhood, my heart and soul wanted to be kind and honorable. I wanted to behave in ways that would provide me experiences that made me feel good about who I was. Despite these desires, I often found myself behaving in ways that provided the ability to get away with things. I acted in ways that helped me fit in and gained acceptance from my peers, regardless of how it made me feel about myself. Rather than following the positive dictates of my heart, I responded to peer pressure. Looking good to others was the common influence and motivator I used to make choices.

The friends and role models I had in my life provided some warped sense of moralities. In some cases, I wonder if most of my friends and mentors had any morality at all. Do not get me wrong, I grew up around some nice people – at least people who were nice to me – as well as some cruel people also. My childhood peers often lacked principles based in honesty about who we wanted to be and what would truthfully make us happy. I've no doubt most of them had good and earnest intentions for the most part. I am sure they simply behaved in the only way they knew.

After high school, I attended a junior college for a few shaky semesters, before dropping out. I had a few go-nowhere jobs, until I discovered my aptitude with computers. I had a knack for keeping my employers happy and figuring out how computer systems worked. With this success, I gained confidence and discovered I am a capable person. I developed an independence from others' and their opinions of me. Over the years, I worked my way into more advanced systems operations, becoming highly qualified in my field, which allowed me to move up into management and larger projects.

I was on my way up the corporate ladder. I was a rising star, one everyone could admire and envy. But I wasn't happy, and at the time I didn't even understand that I was not happy. I was proficient at my career, but I didn't enjoy it. However, like most people, I reminded myself I was making a good living and supporting a family. I pursued and stayed the course for this type of existence no matter how bored and frustrated I became. Not having any understanding that the direction my life was headed would not produce the things I desired.

By the time I approached forty, I had one failed marriage behind me and was twelve years into a second marriage. I had most of the "stuff" that a middle class professional is supposed to want, including material items and the esthetic and emotional beauty found in having a family. But I lacked the peaceful happiness I wanted in my life.

Ten days before my fortieth birthday, an avalanche of change occurred. I lost my career, my marriage, most of the few friends I had. No, I didn't have a mid-life crisis. Rather, I experienced an all too common set of circumstances that is part of many others' biographies. I realized that who I am as a person was not important to those who I was important to. A desire for a new career and all the losses a failed marriage produce left me feeling as if I was starting my adult life all over, from the beginning.

I experienced months of emotional pain, often feeling sorry for myself. My years of marriage had often been filled with frustration and resentment. I'd spent much of my life accepting unacceptable situations in my life, although I'd never understood that or what it meant. All along, many people, including professionals in the fields of sociology and relationships, told me my point of view was delusional. That what I felt should be possible and real is just a delusion.

Finally, with the help of a few friends, I woke from my depression and began to enjoy where I was and who I was in my life. There were choices to be made, including the choice to discover if the dreams and desires, which have always lingered in my soul, had any possibility of being experienced or real. I had the opportunity of finding out if the happiness that I desired to be real and had escaped me all my life could be possible.

As a result of this experience, I began to realize the truths contained in this book, which led to an entirely new point of view and an experience of peace and happiness I'd always thought should be possible, despite a lifetime of being told I must accept what I had is as good as it gets.

Walk with me, to this new point of view. You may disagree with some of my suggestions and discoveries along the way. You may make your own choices about which way to turn. If you do, you may never get the chance to see this view. However, if you stay the course and pursue the directions I provide, you will discover an out look on life that can produce a sense of well being many people only dream of experiencing. Skipping ahead and looking forward in chapters will be a mistake. One truth allows for the next to be understood. This is very important. Understanding basic properties of existence, whether you agree with me or not, allows for a more complete understanding of more complex properties of existence.

This book is not about how to become rich and famous. Neither will monetary wealth assure you happiness or peace, contrary to society's definitions of success.

As a young boy in southern California, I learned many lessons, none of which reflected the truth. I was taught, either directly or through observation, one does whatever is necessary to get what you want. Never admit to anything that would indicate you have faults or ignorance. My life was all about competition, from my family to my friends. Life was not about making someone else feel good, but about making someone else small, so you could feel better about yourself and look better to others. Life was about proving your worth to yourself and others.

The society I lived in – and the society we live in today – is all about winning. If you're not a winner, you're a loser. There is no in-between, or so it seems. The sad truth is, there are very few winners in the world, if we use society's definition. That leaves us with the eventuality the majority of us must be losers. Society is very willing to confirm this idea.

Wrong. The truth is that winning, as defined by society, has nothing to do with happiness. Winning has nothing to do with happiness. Years of observing events and consequences from different points of view have brought me to the conclusion that what we are taught to see as real is simply someone else's misguided truth. Many of the truths we've come to believe are, in fact, false. Granted, many things we think we know are real or truthful. If not, we wouldn't survive at all. But life is more than mere survival and that's where the importance of truth becomes a key to happiness.

Winning. The confusion created by believing this is the key to happiness has led to a great deal of unhappiness, discontent and lack of peace in countless lives. It's led many of us to believe that merely existing is the best we can hope for. This book is written to show you the truth and eliminate the confusion. It's for those of you who come home at the end of a day of work, considered successful in your field, yet feeling your desires and dreams haven't been experienced and never will be. This book is for those who feel money and material items are the way to happiness, yet their wealth hasn't produced experiences that make them feel content or happy. It's for those who feel left behind, because they believe they have no way to buy happiness, no means to create success.

The truth is that everyone, average or amazing, can have the dreams our souls desire and the experiences we desire to enjoy, no matter who we are or how often we've brought home the gold medal or how often we've not even placed in the race of success. We are winners, if we choose to be.

This book will not be politically correct. It is a journey to discover truth and how that truth can lead you to a point of view, which will change your life from mere existence to the realization of dreams and desired experiences. I will state my observations and directions clearly and straightforward. I will call stupidity, stupidity. I will call the best thing to do for you, the best thing to do for you. And I will help you discover why those of you who have no problems persist in thinking life is a problem or life is full of problems, which produce unhappiness and discontent. I live as most of you do. I live with the same simple successes, issues and failures most of you experience. I am not rich. My monetary means are more a struggle than excess.

My life is not the same as it was. It can't be. Once something is added to my knowledge, it becomes a part of me, forever altering what I was before. Parts of me have been broken and have healed, but the scars remain, to remind me of what I experienced and who I've become. Each experience means I've become someone new. Each moment I experience can belong to no one else, whether someone who's come before or will come later. Each moment of my life is unique and special for me and those with whom I experience life.

I cannot be compared to who I was, because I'm no longer that person. Who knows what I will be? The choices I make guide me and provide an idea of who I may become, but I can never say for sure where the path I choose will take me. Based on truth, I live with the willingness to experience my life, no matter what may come, and to take responsibility for experiences of my life and the way I have chosen to experience it. My choices are mine and I can make the choices I desire.

"I wish you the strength and courage to see how your choices affect your experiences."

Thanks, Dix.

CHAPTER ONE

OBSERVATIONS OF TRUTH

I N ORDER TO BE completely confident in what we hold as a
truth, we must have some proof of its validity. Without this
truth, we hold on to some doubt about what we assume is truthful. Doubts have the power to produce many different behavioral
symptoms, most of them negative. Without proof, we live with the
fear others may find out we really don't know the truth, and that
we're making an assumption or taking someone else's word as truth.
Or more likely, that we are simply making-up something that we are
going to state as factual information in order to look like we are an
intelligent valuable person.

Proof can be a direct observation of something. I saw the robin
fly, therefore I can truthfully say robins know how to fly. Proof may
result from deductive reasoning, such as two plus two equals four.
Either way, once we find solid proof, assuring us a thing is truthful,
we're able to relate this understanding to others and ourselves in self-
assured ways, which don't produce doubts and fears we need to hide
from others, to protect our self-esteem.

When I was in the position of hiring others, the most important response I looked for in an interview was an honest and sincere,
"I don't know." I admit I asked unanswerable questions, to see how
a candidate dealt with them. Most of the time, I watched the person
squirm, trying to come up with some type of answer that would
provide an understanding to a fantasy. This signaled the end of the
interview. It indicated to me I couldn't trust the candidate to just
tell me the truth, especially in difficult situations, when the need for
knowing all the facts, as truthfully as possible, was sometimes critical.

Learning the truths for our understandings isn't difficult. The information can be found in many places. With services like the Internet, it's easier than ever to find proof for the information we use to guide our lives.

Unfortunately, many of us find it difficult to check the truthfulness of simple things, much less the more complicated ones. We continue to behave with the same old habits, no matter what the results of these habitual behaviors are. We repeat the same situations over and over again, with the same efforts and behaviors, no matter how many times it turns out in a way we don't desire.

Fear keeps us from admitting to ourselves, and others, that we may not know something. We're afraid others may find out how little we actually understand what comes out of our mouths. We are creatures of habit to the end. We are silly, stubborn humans.

Refusal to face our fears and doubts, in honest and truthful ways, is rampant in our societies. We not only repeat behaviors that don't produce our desired results, we use all our resources and efforts to prove these repeated situations have nothing to do with how we, ourselves, deal with or behave in the situation.

We'd rather look good, by behaving as though we're in the know – even when we have no idea what we're saying – than feel good about something, just by admitting we have no idea if something is true. We dare not be the issue for the aspects of our lives.

It appears most of us are too scared to accept the fact we have the power to make a change, to do something different from that with which we've been comfortable. We've been trained to blame others, rather than take responsibility for how our lives develop. Observation will show you this is common habitual behavior, not a conscious one, and it seldom produces desired results.

This is not all our own faults, for several reasons, one of which is difficult to avoid or correct. This is when we receive untruthful consequences to our behaviors, for whatever reason. Another is our lives limit us to only certain points of view, which hide the truth of a given situation. The most common examples of this are situations in which we accept an understanding provided to us by another person.

Sometimes, people placate us with their responses and observations, in order to be polite. Other times, they give us the same old clichéd answers they've been provided with, although they've never tested or questioned their validity. Sometimes, people just lie.

The most difficult illusion to avoid is when there is more than one possible way to observe a subject, which commonly leaves incomplete observations to be used in determining a complete understanding.

At times, we may observe a situation that seems can only be as we observe it to be, when, more truthfully, the situation may have varying results, all of which are part of the truth. For example, just because all the people you know like a certain type of food, this must mean all people should like it. One cannot prove this true through either limited observation or deduction. Our universe exists with the infinite. Some situations may have more than one truthful understanding.

The saddest part of all this is the fact that those we are closest to, the most important people in our lives, our parents or guardians, provide us with single points of view on subjects and easily convince us this is the full truth. Because we trust them, we don't examine the subjects further, in order to get a more complete understanding of a truth.

Keep your eyes open. It's possible what you want can be experienced, even if everyone you know is telling you it's not. Their experiences may not represent all the possibilities available. This I have observed to be a truth. With one person, an expectation was impossible. With another, it was expected and desired.

The principle of the "observation of truth" is to allow ourselves to think for ourselves. We needn't be held back by having to look like we know something, when we may only have second-hand information about it. This results in a fake existence for who we really are, instead of existing in a truthful existence we desire.

Make no mistake. Humans do desire to know, and look like we know, the truths about how our universe works. When we get what we desire, rather than accepting that which we're taught we should desire, we find joy in and for our lives. There is peace in not having to prove ourselves to others. There is peace in living the truth, in knowing what we know and admitting we don't know what we truly do not know.

Seek the truth and the possibilities of existent become understandable and attainable. Seek the truth and your self-worth becomes greater with each assurance of a truth.

The truth I'm asking you to observe is that which involves how we choose to react to life's stimuli, especially reactions to relationship issues.

If we choose to react based on how other people behave or based on looking good to other people, by reacting with behaviors they think we should choose, we respond habitually, often with like behaviors, we surrender the power we have to create our desired existence. Nastiness is responded to with nastiness, for example. These choices are not benefiting us or leading us to the experiences we desire in life. If we only react lovingly when loving is provided to us, we are giving up any control or influence we possess to guide our lives to our desired experiences. A life based on truth allows you to make choices about your reactions, based on what you want, not on how someone or something else is behaving.

"We hold these truths to be self-evident," states our nation's constitution. Some truths have very little proof to support them, but often can be observed and found as truth from the self-evidence they provide. Much of what is in this book has very little proof, except that when observed it can be defined as truth, as it is self-evident. Those in this world who deny that, "All men are created equal, that they are endowed by their Creator with certain unalienable Rights, that among these are Life, Liberty and the Pursuit of Happiness," lack the ability to observe truth. Anyone who cannot observe the truthfulness in the proclamation set forth by the founding fathers of the United States is in denial.

It's clear that freedom for the human soul to explore and experience life, as well as the protection and enforcement of such liberties, has provided a nursery for the greatest evolution of mankind. This evolution has inspired the greatest of possibilities, by providing imagination and ideas a place where they are allowed to develop and grow. It's provided a place to better understand and eliminate confusion, by factually discovering the truth, as well as providing a sanctuary for questioning that which is proclaimed as truth, allowing for discoveries that can produce a more honest and righteous existence.

"I am, therefore I exist," is truth.

"I feel pain, therefore I hurt," is truth.

Evidence can be provided for proof of such statements. However, physical proof is not a necessity to understand the truth in all statements. Some things are self-evident. If the way I interact and behave produces a more joyful existence for me or someone else, the cause and affect can be observed and little proof is necessary. If the way I choose to experience the world brings me peace, the peace I feel in my life is all the proof necessary to show me my choice is better than other choices I've made which didn't produce such peace.

To say that I'm not pleased with the way my life is going and/ or my life is causing me grief is to say my life's choices, behaviors and experiences are not founded in truth. I've observed this statement to be self-evident. A false life produces confusion, which creates the stress and frustrations, which lead to unhappiness.

As you can see, I don't talk in analytical terms or pretend I can psychoanalyze any mental issues. I write in normal and simple common language, for it is all I know how to do. I hope to provide an explanation of what I've observed as the driving forces of human nature, from the core of our being. Mental illness and physical mental issues are for professionals, trained to deal with them. The ideas within this book are from my own observations of life and are meant to help the average and normal person understand some basic principles for coping with, dealing with, life.

The point of view I wish to share with you is about dealing with the negative consequences and situations in our lives, which are produced by the choices we make. I want to provide and explain a process to help you determine what choices are best for your existence, what choices will allow for the possibilities of experiencing your desires for life.

Most choices that cause us problems or unhappiness are those we make when it comes to some type of human relationship. Whether the relationship is spousal, family, friendship, business or our personal relationship with ourselves, how we react to situations in the relationships is our choice. If you are, in any way, unsatisfied with how you're experiencing your life and you find it comes from some type of relationship concerns, it just may be a result of choices. It may be the way you choose to see, be affected by and react to the situations in your life, especially in your relationships.

CHAPTER TWO

THE PHYSICS OF EXISTENCE

THE PHYSICS OF EXISTENCE is more than just the science of physics, although the science of physics is a part of the physics of existence. Our existence is made up of four elements: the physical, spiritual, emotional and intellectual.

The physical element is obvious and being constantly studied. Physics has taught us one very important truth. Laws govern existence. It is not within our power to change, create or destroy these laws. We may manipulate our environment, by manipulating the laws of existence, but we are at the mercy of these laws.

Although physics is the study of natural science, it is also the general analysis of nature. There is more to our existence than the tangible or physical. When it comes to our existence, we have to admit that if something exists, it must exist with a set of laws, whether these come from accidental chaos or purpose.

Our existence can be broken down into a few simple subjects: the physical, the spiritual and the connection between the physical and spiritual. Each of these has laws that govern them.

It is simple enough to determine that physical things exist. To touch them, to experience them in different ways, is all we need to understand that physical things are all around us. Science has studied and discovered many truths and supposed truths of our physical universe.

Often, we rely on religion to explain the truths or supposed truths regarding our spirit. However, finding consistent laws of the spirit from the dogma and doctrine of religion is pretty unreliable, although I have observed that finding truth within faith is a viable possibility.

The idea that we know we exist is the spirit existing. One law of existence would have to be the Law of Self Awareness, since all healthy humans live within this knowledge. Even though the law has no tangible properties, it still exists. This means the Laws of Physics or Natural Science must include more than just the tangible and the material. This is what I define as the Physics of Existence, encompassing the physical, spiritual, emotional and intellectual.

As stated above, the physical is pretty obvious and there are experts more qualified than I to discuss this element. The basic understanding of the physical universe is that it is the place in which all things manifest and become real and the manifestation of our dreams and desires within this universe is very important.

Although the Physics of Existence includes the physical, it is the spirit and the connection between the physical and spirit, which will be emphasized in this book, providing ideas on how to best exist so the spirit achieves its deepest desires and experience.

We'll also discuss the intellect, because without the tool of our intellect, this would all be wasted paper. The intellectual element is the tool we use to understand the physical universe and it can provide logical or creative understandings for our existence.

The emotional element is the tool our spirit uses to communicate with our physical and intellectual elements. The spirit is the underlying motivator for our desires.

This is the basis for how we exist in this universe. It sounds simple. I don't believe it was meant to be complicated. The diagram on the next page shows you the simple integration of the elements.

In this diagram, we see how the spirit is in place to communicate with and experience our universe, through the intellect and the physical body. The triangle represents the physical body where emotional language is used to communicate between the intellectual, physical and spirit elements. This is the basic structure of our existence. The intellect gathers data from physical stimuli: site, sound, smell, taste and touch (touch also being the ability to feel or sense vibrations of energy).

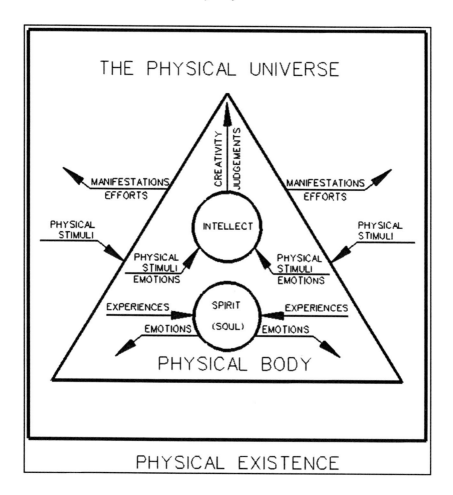

Our physical bodies experience our physical universe. Our intellect reasons information and makes judgments and provides creative possibilities. Our soul, or spirit, demands experiences (or purpose, if you wish). Our emotions provide communication between the other elements of existence. Understanding the laws for each individual element provides the resources for us to achieve our desires.

If we misunderstand what an emotion is trying to tell us, which we often do, or if we misinterpret what emotions really are, we receive no benefit for or from a truthful physical element of existence. Emotions exist, although they may use chemical processes to manifest their existence. The existence of things created by purpose or natural selection is seldom useless. In fact, my observations show me they are never useless.

Just as the belief the earth was flat provided people with useless conclusions, the idea of believing sadness is a bad and useless chemical process has the same affect. Emotions have specific reasons. Observations conclude they are important and useful communications from our souls.

I wish I could explain all this in a simple, ten word sentence, but it's not that simple. However, the principle is simple. Existence can be what you want, if you're willing to accept the truth about what you want.

CHAPTER THREE

THE PHYSICS OF SPIRIT

E RNEST HOLMES, AUTHOR OF the book Science of the Mind, teaches us that the spiritual, mental and emotional world has laws, just like the science of physics. These laws are impersonal. These laws hold no preference for one person or another. They just exist. If understood, they can be used to create a more fulfilling life.

I like to compare the physical properties of laws to the spiritual, mental and emotional properties of laws. So you understand references I make, you need to know that, for me, the words Nature, God and Universe are synonymous. Whenever one of these words is used in this book, understand I am referencing all of them and you may see it from whatever point of view that works for your existence.

I have observed the laws of Nature, God and/or the Universe, whether it is a physical, spiritual, mental or emotional laws all have a common principle. These laws exist and we have no control over how they exist. They exist in a constant state and do not change from influences within our existence and universe. The laws don't care who understands them and uses them for benefit or loss. They don't have the ability to choose, change or belong to anyone. They cannot choose those they wish to benefit. They have no ability to change. They cannot be owned. The laws of nature are impersonal. Laws of the universe work the way they work. We can only manipulate a law under its conditions. It's never possible to change the properties of a law.

The more we understand the laws of nature and how they work, the more we're able to use them to our benefit. The less willing we are to seek this truth, the more we deny it as a truth, the more we believe we can make the universe the way we want it to be, the greater the odds are against living a peaceful, desired existence.

This doesn't mean we have no control or influence to shape our reality and experiences. Quite the opposite. The laws of our universe are very basic building blocks and the creative processes to manipulate these laws belong to sentient beings, such as humans. The possibilities for creative manipulation of the laws of the universe are infinite. Although the laws of nature do not change, we can use these laws to produce change for our benefit or loss. Taking this one step further, since there are infinite possibilities for creation within these laws of the universe, it can be deduced all situations have the possibility to be changed, for benefit or loss.

Let's look at an example of how using the physics of nature, the physical and tangible part of existence, can be used or ignored to produce the success or failure of a desired experience.

Let's say I decide to be a farmer and grow crops to benefit the world and, hopefully, make enough money to at least break even for my efforts. Let's also say I'm a delusional person and believe my goodness is all I need to reap an abundant crop, because I've been taught that being kind and good is the best way to reap success.

I purchase a piece of land, paying no attention to the quality of the soil, access to water or issues of seasons and weather for the location. I purchase some seed that has the ability to produce food for humans. I truck the seed to my land and spend days throwing the seed onto the dry and nutrient barren soil. I spend the next six months being as generous and kind as I can. However, I put no efforts into attending to my fields.

I planted my crop in the late fall in a northern latitude. I never watered the fields or tilled the soil or made sure the seeds were beneath the soil. I never checked for pests or weeds. I prayed to my God and asked for a bountiful harvest. All my acquaintances testify I'm a very good and kind person, who deserves the best in life, because of the way I treat others and the fact I stand by my convictions, promises and word. I am praised as trustworthy and fun to be around by all who know me.

Months later, I walk out to my fields and find them barren. The laws of nature have not cared about me as a person. They don't have that ability. They just exist in the manner for which they exist. I did not seek the truth about my situation, nor did I acquaint myself with the laws of nature. As a result, I have failed at producing a bountiful harvest. The reasons why are obvious to everyone but me.

I could make excuses or blame various people or issues for my failure, but the truth is the only one to blame is myself and it's possible I'm not at fault either. If I didn't know better, how could I be at fault?

However, if the knowledge of how to do better was easily accessible and I had some understanding that information was readily available to help me with the situation, then I was only being foolish in my efforts and considerations of the truths, if I don't accept the failure as being my choice, because I didn't seek the truth.

Certain situations are often new to our understanding and access to accurate and helpful information on a new subject may not exist. In cases such as these, I may fail in my effort, without having the need to judge my truth and quality of effort. Since the infinite exists, it's possible to make an effort for some given subject, considering all possible and available information, and still find some new, unforeseen issue that may cause less than the desired goals. It's possible the information I was provided or sought was false and misleading. Regardless, seeking the truth about the laws of the universe puts the odds greatly in my favor to succeed at my efforts. For me, this idea seems obvious and self-evident.

Now, let's look at the same desire to produce a crop, but this time we'll use the physics of nature.

I first educate myself on what crops yield the most produce from their growth and market place. I select a crop that is not only financially lucrative, but one that has proven to be hardy, with the ability to survive various environmentally difficult conditions. I do adequate research to determine desirable locations for the purchase of land, based on the most advantageous seasonal and weather conditions for the crop. I search for options in suitable locations, which can be purchased for the lowest possible amounts. Before making a purchase, I hire a soil expert to assure the quality of soil on the land I'm considering will suit my purposes. I determine whether added nutrients may be of benefit. I research any possible concerns of flora or fauna that may exist in the region I plan to plant.

Before ever starting the project, I make the effort to seek out as much known truth about it as is prudent. I work within the understanding of observed positive results of the laws that govern the growth of the crop. I plant the seeds, tend the soil, water and fertilize, all based on the needs of the crop. I make an effort to understand the basic genetic possibilities for producing a more advantageous yield.

I do not pray or even acknowledge a power greater than nature itself. I rely only on science and intellect. Most of the people I encounter consider me rude and selfish. I provide nothing to charity and could care less about the needs of the world. I'm willing to use chemicals to help me achieve my goals, despite the fact they may have harmful affects on the ecology. My character and personality are of no concern to me. I live in my own selfish bubble. We could easily define me as a nasty and grumpy person.

Nonetheless, months later, I have an outstanding crop, have recovered all my investment and made a profit.

Why? The laws of nature dealing with the aspects of my agricultural project have no understanding, no idea nor any concern about how good or nice a person I may be. Because I understood these laws, I could use them to my benefit. I do not control the laws of nature, but I understand them, which allows me to make choices, which will benefit my crop and almost assure success. The laws are impersonal to any other issues, such as my nature and character.

Before you draw conclusions about the above two scenarios, notice how each has success and failure within it. That is because the laws of nature extend to the spirit, as well as the physical. Testing and observation have shown this idea to be true.

In the first case, the physics of the tangible were ignored, but the physics of the spirit were addressed. In the second case, the physics of the spirit were ignored, while the physics of the tangible were addressed. In either case, if we do not educate ourselves to the truth about the laws of the universe, the odds against success for our efforts become almost insurmountable.

While it is difficult to come to terms with, the fact is our goodness may not have anything to do with whether or not we are successful in our efforts.

While I've observed prayer may enlighten us to ideas and knowledge, I've never observed an act of direct intervention, thought to have come from a greater being, which doesn't have some other possible explanation, easily understood within the laws of our universe.

I have observed that prayer does have power. It can be used to our service. However, there's no ability for a greater power to reach into our universe from an outside source and defy the laws of our universe. If a greater power or being actually created our universe, and in doing so established the laws of our universe, it would be subject to the laws that it created, even if it came from another place of existence. Its nature would be bound to the same rules as yours and mine.

Think about it. Any small change in the physical properties of our universe would change existence as we experience it, thereby creating a different awareness for existence. It may be possible for someone or something to play with the laws of this universe, but doing so would mean altering the current awareness of this universe's existence.

One of the most popular acts of intervention by a greater being is the immaculate conception of Jesus Christ. A woman is professed to have become pregnant, without ever having sexual relations with any man. Thousands of years ago, even less than a hundred years ago, this could be explained as a miracle, performed through some act of a great power, understood by no one.

Today, it's easy to understand how a woman could become pregnant without ever having sexual relations with a man. I'm not trying to answer questions about miracles with this example. I'm just using it to portray the possibilities for understandable explanations for non-understood acts in our universe. What we don't understand today may become commonly held knowledge tomorrow.

I am not refuting or supporting the existence of a creator or a greater power or being. I'm only trying to show that, however this universe came into existence, we are at its mercy. From all my observations, I've come to understand that, purposely or by accident, the universe we are a part of is subject to the properties of its laws.

Imagine what would happen if the basic properties of matter – neutrons, protons and electrons – were changed. Just one small change in this physical law would destroy all that is, at least as we know it. Although something might still exist in its place, our awareness of this existence would change, along with the change of properties of matter. You and I would no longer exist.

The Law of Free Will and God is one of my favorite subjects. It is so beautiful, so wonderful and truly easy to understand. Free will is what allows for possibilities beyond any singular point of view, even that of the Creator. With the gift of free will, the infinite is possible. There are no limitations to what can be, other than those that come from our own desire for them to exist. Free will is the law that permits choice for positive or negative results. Even the physical properties of our universe have free will. This is why the universe isn't perfect and often produces undesirable results. Free will allows for anything to be possible, within the laws of this universe.

Lets explore some ideas. It's often a practice to praise and glorify not only a Creator's existence and/or holiness, but the command the Creator holds over wondrous knowledge and understanding. However, if a being is alone in its existence or lives in a world of absolutes, with no relativity to allow for comparison of opposing ideas to exist, how does one judge an idea? How does one determine what is truly wonderful and wondrous and what just is, if there's nothing else to compare it to?

If I am a great, powerful and all-able being and I experience a desire to be praised for my greatness, it's a simple thing to just create an infinite hoard of beings, who will sit around and tell me how great I am. But, is this anything more than self-acknowledgment being proliferated, without any truth or any understanding of what being great is? This greater being might as well be humming praises to itself. Puppets have no way of seeking the truth and can only do what their masters command.

If I want to know the difference between one thing and another, greatness or ordinary, I must have a place where it's possible for things to be judged and measured. Without relativity, there is no better or worse. There can be no greatness, if there is no smallness. We live in a reality that is in a relative universe. We have the ability to compare and judge aspects of existence.

Free will allows the possibility for ideas, opinions and thoughts to be unique and genuine points of view, which have the ability to create new possibilities, expand understandings and create ideas that can be compared, measured and judged. Without free will, there is no way to seek proof for truth. We wouldn't be able to discover the how and why, nor determine the quality or value of such discoveries.

Free will is, and must be, absolute or it isn't free will. This is the only truthful understanding I've found for why our universe is capable of such wonderful beauty and, yet, can create comparable suffering. It's not the desire or act of anyone or anything to produce horrible experiences. It's only the nature of how it must be, in order to understand the idea of something being wonderful.

Without the horror, there can be no understanding of peace. A creator of such a thing has no choice, but to let it exist without direct intervention into the laws of its existence. To intervene in the free will of the existence of a thing is to take away its freedom, thereby destroying its ability to be as it has always been, free to exist. Without free will, you could never truly be judged by anything other than yourself.

Relative reality allows for the judgment of quality, free will always for a way to prove truth does exist for a judgment. This is the law of our universe. This law dictates how the universe works, not because of some being's desire, but because this is the only way a relative reality can exist.

Free will is a synonym for the infinite. Free will allows for no limitations, just as the infinite allows for no limitations. We live in a universe where the infinite is possible and real.

Free will is a law and must be a law of our universe. Either free will exists, as does the horror that comes with it, or it doesn't exist and allows for all horror to be eliminated.

Without free will, possibility would have limits. With free will, infinite possibilities are unlimited. This makes it possible to experience unlimited joy and pleasure. Maybe this can comfort those who find it hard to understand why suffering and horror must exist. They exist to allow for an unlimited, erotic existence to exist.

CHAPTER FOUR

CONFUSION

I HAVE OBSERVED ONE common behavior that hinders humans from obtaining their dreams of what they feel life should be like. It is the defensive behaviors we use to protect ourselves, not from physical threats, but from fear of others judgments of our quality and worth. We fear others will somehow find out we're confused about why life isn't offering the experiences we desire and have no idea how to change this situation. To add to our confusion, we're often informed life cannot and will not produce the experiences we desire from our existence.

In the field of physics, there is a theory for singularity, the one property of the physical universe to which all physical law can be traced. The idea that all physical theories and laws should trace back conclusively to the singularity is the core to proving such physical properties are true.

Some may think it strange that I'm willing to point to the singularity in human behavior, given the following. We, as humans, understand so little about human behavior. With our mass of understanding of the physical universe, the physical singularity is still being pondered.

When I observe human behavior, I find it possible to trace the cause for most issues and distress back to one singular point. Confusion. If you think of human thought and emotion as elements, you can think of confusion as a reaction to the lack of truthful understanding of such elements as thoughts and emotions. The stimulus of our intellect, which comes from the elements of thoughts and emotions, is information, but not summation of that information. Without being able to determine that we know which choices can produce the existence we desire to experience, we have no way of eliminating the confusion surrounding any choice we make, beneficial or detrimental.

Whether the reaction or consequences between thoughts and emotions result in beneficial experiences or not doesn't provide an understanding of confusion. The knowledge to determine how choices affect our existence is understanding. This understanding eliminates confusion.

Imagine being in a fully stocked kitchen and asked to bake a cake. If you don't have a recipe or the knowledge of how to bake a cake, all the materials in the world aren't going to produce the desired result, unless it occurs totally by accident. And accidents still result in confusion. We can have an accidental experience of what we desire, but not know how or why it occurred.

From what I've observed, confusion can be one of the greatest hindrances to a happy, complete and joyful existence. Confusion can most often be traced back to our childhood. From an early age, we're told what to think, how to feel, what is and is not important for a happy and successful life.

Have you told your children, or been told by your parents, that Santa Clause, the Easter bunny or the Boogeyman exists?

How many times have you heard, "My ship will come in," or "God will provide," or "If only I had...?"

Have you been told you don't feel the way you feel?

"You can't be cold. It's eighty degrees."

"You can't be hungry. You just ate."

We're told so many simple things in our lives by important role figures, such as parents, teachers and friends. Their pronouncements make us reevaluate what we already knew as truth. At first, we trust without thought, but then we discover so many of these are false.

I'm cold, if I feel cold. I'm hungry, if I feel hungry. There is no Santa Clause. I know no one whose ship has come in.

Soon, we stopped trusting what these mentors told us. Soon, we recognize it doesn't take a human long to begin defending positions of understanding that we know aren't true or that we believe have the possibility of not being true, in order to maintain the appearance of being proficient in our lives.

This is immensely confusing. The people you trust the most in your life have been providing you information that doesn't add up.

Have you ever wondered why a child becomes irritated, rebellious, sad, depressed or angry? Imagine how you'd feel, if a very important person in your life was supporting fairy tales. This same person is telling you how you feel is, should or could never be possible. He or she, this person who has authority over your life, is trashing your dreams of how you truthfully feel and what you truthfully desire, while lying to you.

Ask your children why they have negative behaviors and you'll most likely find they have no answers nor any way of articulating the reasons for such behaviors. This is due to lack of education in the ability to understand their conflicts. This lack leaves them unable to understand and results in confusion and frustration, which leads to embarrassment for not knowing if their choices in life will produce what they want to experience. Human nature is to avoid embarrassment, to avoid looking bad. This is what produces defensive behaviors, which we use to defend our weaknesses.

Let's get even more basic. Ask a child who they are and what they want to be. They'll likely answer by telling you their name and stating an occupation. The name was given to them and the dream of an occupation is usually based on information provided them by a third party. As parents, we often guide our children into choices and ideas we feel are good choices for us. How can we say our choices in life are good choices for our children, or anyone else, for that matter?

Have you experienced your dreams for your life? If you have, maybe you can be a good guide for someone else. If you have not, it's blind arrogance to insist you know what choices will produce desired experiences for someone else.

Let's get more personal. Who are you and what do you want to be?

I don't mean what is your name and what do you do for a living. Beyond those two standard answers, most of us find it difficult to define who we are, even to ourselves. Yet, we go around trying to explain ourselves to others and, often, trying to help others define themselves.

This is the beginning, the foundation, of confusion. Most of us have no idea how to define ourselves. We run around living life as defined by someone or something else, at best. At worst, we just live our lives in one big accidental experience. We make choices based on confused understandings of life, rather than choices based on what we desire to experience in our existence.

This has never made me happy. I've found the mentoring I've received from others is more often false than based in factual, observed truth. Even when others present the truth, it's often accidental and not tested, merely regurgitated information, which leaves us confused by why or how such information could be truthful. Without proof or understanding of truth, it's difficult to find peace in why something can be truthful or to trust at all that a truthful fact is actually fact. This simply creates more confusion.

If you can define who and what you are or, better yet, who and what you'd like to be, the confusion surrounding the determination of what are the better choices for you to make in your life will be reduced, sometimes greatly reduced. With the knowledge of who and what you want to be, you can make choices that produce the experiences you desire easier to define, understand and prove. This makes you much more confident about the choices you make and removes or reduces confusion. You're then much more assured and less concerned about any need to defend your understandings of life. You do understand and don't need to only pretend.

I've observed that people seldom get angry or frustrated when defending a position or issue they know is correct. I've also observed that most frustration comes from defending situations we only think are the truth, for which we have no supporting observation or information. The desire to conform to society's judgments of us often leads us to choices, which will provide acceptance. These choices often conflict with the truths that would produce our desires, thus confusing us and creating doubts that destroy our peace of mind.

Imagine you're going on a trip. You've gathered all the tools you need to get to where you'd like to go: a car, maps of the world, money, snacks, etc. You hop in the car and start driving. The problem is, you have no idea where you're going. You wander aimlessly, with no idea how to get to where you'd like to be, because you have no idea where you want to go. You may see beautiful sights, as you drive, thinking the trip is great. However, without a lot of luck, you may end up out of supplies and fuel, in some desolate place, without any idea of how to get some place better and no resources to make the attempt. We all know the odds on being lucky are astronomically against us.

Most choices of turns or direction will be a guess, with little or no confidence in the correctness of these choices leading us on the desired course to the desired destination. You can willingly admit, at each choice, you have no idea which choice is best or you can illogically defend the choice, claiming you do have some idea where you're going. This often makes one look like an ass. Since society is willing to label someone who has little confidence in their understandings of existence as a lower class of person, this results in a self-image of low esteem, producing all sorts of negative symptoms.

Life is the journey you're on and most of us have no idea where we want to go. Life, as a journey, has few permanent destinations, but having some idea of which direction to take, to achieve your desires, and what it takes to get there is a good idea. It's pretty confusing, not understanding what you need to know and do to get what it is you want.

Life demands enough decisions that require us to muddle through possible consequences, which often produce confusion when we know where it is we want to go. Not having any idea of what the journey is or how to determine what it's about leaves you with little possibility of having confidence in the choices you make. This is the confusion that leads to problems. I've observed that most of us have no idea what will truly make us happy and what will produce a more fulfilled existence.

Eliminate your confusion over daily decision and major decisions by figuring out who and what you want to be. With this information, you're armed with a roadmap of what choices will get you to the place you desire to be.

It is possible for some people to accidentally find their way down the path of making choices, based on who and what they want to be, not paying any attention to how to get there. It's also possible someone will win the lottery this week. Most of us, however, need to educate ourselves and learn to eliminate the confusion, in order to find our way.

Many very happy people live lives with these ideals, whole or in part, knowing or not knowing, enjoying a very productive and highly fulfilling existence. All I'm saying is that understanding the causes that produce effects arms us with tools to make life even more productive. Even the most complete and accomplished people can benefit from having a more specialized set of power tools to get the job done.

Although this may be as much a leap of faith as an observed insight into human nature, I've observed that confusion is the one thing from which come all of life's frustrations, depression, negative rebellions and misunderstood anger. These negative emotions and situations diminish the desire for experiencing life, by supporting the notions that life isn't or may never be what we desire to experience. They provide opportunities for situations that progressively exacerbate the lack of hope that life has any possibility of measuring up to our desires.

Confusion creates fear. Not knowing, not being sure of the choices we make, in order to select the appropriate efforts necessary, in order to look good to others, scares us. Because we're scared, we hide this attribute of our existence with all the intellect we have. We spend our entire lives defending something we know we don't know, in order to never admit we don't know what we're doing. As a result, stupid situations, arguments and moronic efforts confuse us even more, in a world we're trying to figure out.

The efforts we put into looking good to others are a waste, when all we want is to be good to ourselves. We can never fully satisfy others' expectations of what we're taught we should be. Life becomes an endless cycle of effort, due to an infinite possibility of expectations.

If you're confused over this type of life, because it's not working for you, it's an obvious observation it will never produce the experiences you desire from life. Don't try and figure it out. Leave it behind and forget it. Try to eliminate the confusion by making choices for what you feel you want to experience. This is difficult to do and is taught in very limited forums. When we don't do this, we often live with the double whammy of confusion on how to satisfy the world and satisfy our being.

We can eliminate a huge part of our confusion by simply stopping our efforts to satisfy other's expectations and starting to focus on the efforts we can make to satisfy what we desire to experience in this existence. Let me be clear. When we make choices based on what we want to be, this is not about not caring about the world. If we want to be a caring person, we need to make choices based on what it is that makes us a caring person.

I know a couple that are having some bad marital issues early in their marriage. From my viewpoint, they had issues before they got married. The wife comes to our house to get away from her husband and chat about the issues. The usual stuff is discussed. "He does this. How can I live with that? What should I do when he..."

All I can say is she needs to stop making choices based on her husband's behaviors. The only advice I can give her is to make choices based on who and what she wants to be. If you want to be this type of wife, be this. If you want to be that type of wife, be that. Just because her husband is an ass, does it make her happy or bring her joy to be something she doesn't want to be, simply as a response to his behavior? When you're happy with who you are, through making choices based on who you want to be, someone else's behavior seldom affects how you feel. Simply put, I am happy; if you're a dork, that's your problem.

I'll be discussing simple ideas and practical ways to understand and apply how to make choices based on who you want to be. I'll also provide exercises to easily discover how to define what is most important to you or who you want to be. I can't define what someone else desires from their existence as well as that person can do for themselves. Hopefully, these ideas and exercises will eliminate the majority of confusion that hinders our abilities to experience our existence in a manner we desire. This approach has worked for me, and others I've observed.

CHAPTER FIVE

TRUTH

THE LAW OF TRUTH: Truth is what is. We may not feel or agree with the truth, but it is still the truth. Use the truth to make your life what you desire it to be.

So many important people in my life have asked me why I think truth is so important. Because the idea of truth seems so simple to me, it's difficult for me to understand and live with the idea that others find it such a difficult concept. I can say, without hesitation, that I find people who do not search for truth to be offensive and lacking in intelligence of any quality. I know this may sound extremely judgmental. It is. However, I've been victimized by false actions and beliefs of the world, as well as my own. The distress and pain it has caused me has left me lacking pity and understanding for those who harm others by living false lives.

Falsifying truth, for the benefit of your own personal gain, embarrassment and/or fear, is seldom a victimless action. There is consequence to any and all actions. Physics teaches us every action has an equal or opposite reaction.

I find that I'm embarrassed by my need for judgment. The emotion of embarrassment is a feeling that tells us either we don't have the ability to accept something or the respectful ability to correct something. With this in mind, I am taking action to inform others of my observations, in hopes of helping to correct, in some way, the confusion with which so many of us live.

Let's go back to the original thought of how so many others can dismiss the understanding of how truth can better our lives. Imagine scenarios where truth isn't provided and see how most of the consequences of such actions can cause discord. Truth may not always be easy and may not always produce peace, but it does allow for assured decisions and is the only true way to alleviate confusion.

The truth is, very few of us have any idea of what truth actually is. Today's attitude is that truth has little to do with finding happiness. Instead, we live in a tangible world and the more things we have, the better our lives will be.

I've observed this condition to be one that is unintentional and undesired, although our society stresses this understanding. I'm not making a judgment of character for most people, but a judgment of our habitual behaviors. I am here to proclaim that once love is found and life is safe, truth is the only thing left that has any affect on our well being.

From the beginning of our lives, we are lied to and taught how to lie. We're educated in fantasies. We soon begin deluding ourselves into believing the lies we tell ourselves. We put faith in a world deluded by fantasies, believing fantasy has an ability to produce happiness. My observations show fantasies do not produce happiness. I've also observed no spiritual text denies the importance of truthful knowledge. In fact, any spiritual writings I've read emphasize that truthful knowledge is of extreme importance for any understanding.

In science, there is a process called the Scientific Theorem. This is used to determine whether a postulated suggestion can be proven true. In this process, it's necessary to be able to observe any suggested theorem, in order to determine whether it can contain truth. Science doesn't simply take someone's word that any suggestion is true. It must be provable.

Unfortunately, as humans in today's society, we take information from almost any source as truth, without any proof.

Webster defines truth, as a noun, to mean "conformity to fact; that which is true." He defines true as an adjective, meaning "faithful to reality, real, genuine or dependable." I've observed these words to be very important in the pursuit of happiness.

As stated earlier, I've observed that man's most common issue with emotional, spiritual and mental contentment is confusion. What can be more confusing than trying to make a decision, based on false information? Yet, we seldom do anything to prove and support most of the information provided to us in our lives.

Why not simply observe? Question what you're told, until an observation of truth presents itself. Be open to possibilities without fear. Be able and willing to say, "I don't know," or "I'm not sure, but let's see if we can find the truth."

I know this isn't as simple as it sounds. The world in which we live doesn't teach us to do this. Most of what I've been taught is simply to be like others and accept their definition of what is truth.

Although it's not the only ingredient for happiness and it's only a word, it's the first place to look for all that is real. Happiness is real, and must be real, for it to exist at all.

Truth and trust are requirements for relationships to work, but I'm more concerned with truth as a guide for the way in which we live life for ourselves. If we were to believe we can breathe under water, without any tools or apparatus to assist us, we'd find ourselves sucking water into our lungs, in an effort to breath.

While this may seem obvious and ludicrous, we tend to live our lives in such obvious ludicrousness. Instead of admitting we're wrong or we don't know, we fight to be seen as correct or "in the know." In fact, most of the time, most of us haven't the foggiest idea of what we're excreting from our mouths.

It's not entirely our fault truth eludes us. What we believe to be truth has been taught to the majority of us from the beginning of our existence. Our parents, teachers, family members, friends and society regurgitate the same old false ideas for happiness they were taught. Seldom do we question these teachings, much less admit they could possibly be wrong.

Why? Because we must win. We must not look bad. We must get good grades, run faster, score more points and beat the person next to us. The more often we beat them, the better it is. The more we have than someone else, the better our lives should be.

The price we pay to be a winner is enormous. Check out the money spent on professional sports. I don't think there's anything wrong with professional sports and I believe healthy competition makes a valuable contribution to our existence. It's just that beating someone at some sort of competition has seldom, if ever, had anything to do with happiness.

This is how most of us are taught to behave. Have you ever really considered whether this will make you live a better life? Have you ever considered that you've never been taught how to be happy or what happiness is? Have you ever questioned what you've been taught?

Maybe it's time we grow and evaluate what's real, what works and what makes us happy as mature adults. Maybe it's time we stop accepting what we've been told and what we've been taught to believe as truth by others.

I'm not saying those who've introduced us to false information are necessarily at fault nor am I judging their character. In fact, I've observed regurgitating false information has nothing to do with character. It has to do with behavior.

Most behaviors are learned habits, often undesired and unproductive behaviors and habits. Fortunately, our behaviors and habits can be easily corrected. Habitual behaviors seldom portray their true character. Character is a conscious choice. Character is about how we behave and act, not about what we think, whether we choose to be guided by our character or not. It must be a conscious choice, in order for us to truly know our character is able to provide us with self-worth. To find peace and enjoy our lives, we need to feel confident and not be confused, through questioning our choices. Only through seeking the truth can we eliminate the confusion of not knowing the best choices for our desired existence.

Truth is based in the laws of the universe. Physics, for example, is based in truth. Knowing more about the truth of physics allows us to have a better understanding of how the universe works, providing us the opportunity to use this information to our benefit.

What makes the emotional, mental and spiritual aspects of the universe any different than the physics of the universe? There are laws regarding each aspect of the spirit, just as there are laws in physics. Building your life on false laws, such as the belief the world is flat, hinders your ability to live a happier life. The first law to all aspects is that any law must be truthful.

Allowing ourselves to live by truthful laws of the intellect and spirit, means we can construct behaviors that use these laws to our benefit. I've observed the understanding of the laws of the intellect and spirit can produce an amazing existence, one I can only define as erotic, in terms of the type of exstence life provides me in everything I do.

CHAPTER SIX

EXPERIENCE

WHILE EXPERIENCE IS GOOD, it's another one of those things that gets in our way. On one hand, experience gives you an edge to do better. On the other hand, it makes you aware of options, which makes it more difficult to be content and happy with where you are or what you have. Not all experiences produce useful or truthful understandings or abilities.

Imagine never having anything to eat, except beans. Beans are all you've known and beans taste great when you're hungry. If you have a craving to eat, you simply go get some beans. Life is simple. There are no choices you need to make for what you may desire or need when you're hungry.

Imagine that one day you get to eat a great steak dinner with all the trimmings, including good wine and a delicious desert. While something in this meal may not appeal to your underdeveloped palate, I'm sure your body will find many of the food items extremely pleasing, if not for the luxury, for the high nutritional value.

Life will forever be changed for you. You now know a choice exists to satisfy your hunger and it's possible to acquire different types of food. New cravings, more specific than just hunger, will now emerge. With those cravings come possible feelings of frustration, when a craving can't be fulfilled.

The experience of new and better things produces more knowledge, which must be dealt with. Our minds and souls must find ways to live with this new information and the issues that come with trying to satisfy multiple choices. The body now craves more nutritional satiation, simply because of one small gourmet meal in a lifetime of meals.

We have more choices available to us than I can count, which provides the necessity of choosing, in order to exist. Confusion is just a part of the nature of experience in our relative universe. Learning how to deal with confusion and choices may be a good idea.

Let's look at reality and the choices we know we have, from all the experiences we've had. Tastes, feelings, smells, influences and comforts all come with choices. Our experiences not only add to our possible choices, but also assign qualities to those choices. Not only does what we've experienced cause us mental and emotional pause, so does the act of choosing. In addition to considering the possibility of various choices, we have the difficulty of choosing something, which will produce the experience we desire at that moment.

Look at the choice we make when we choose a monogamous commitment to a mate. When I first started dating, as a young man, I was willing to accept certain characteristics in my mate, characteristics I had little experience with. I assumed I just needed to live with what I chose and make the best of it. In fact, I found little reason for any issue but satisfaction, because I wasn't aware of any other possibilities.

After years of experience and dating a greater number of women, I found I had preferences and desires for specific characteristics in partners. Certain characteristics, which once were completely acceptable and thought of as pleasurable, became issues for decisions. This made it harder to find a satisfactory partner, one with whom I could be satisfied and joyfully happy, because it was more difficult to find a single person who completed all the choices I've discovered about what I desire in my life.

Think about all the times you've been hungry and gone to a fine restaurant. You look at the extensive menu and everything sounds wonderful. A single choice is difficult. Heck, I used to order two entries. However, we can only eat so much, before we feel sick and overfed. A choice must be made from all the possibilities.

Life is filled with possibilities. Knowing which ones are best for your life is the key to success. Eliminating the confusion over what is most important and productive for you is the key to a simpler existence of mental and emotional satisfaction. Life is anything but simple. It's not meant to be anything simple. Life is a challenge of choices. I'd much rather have the choices I know I have, and many more I'll learn are possible, despite the fact they make me ponder, think and worry, than have no choice at all and live with limited experiences.

We rarely think twice about the simple choices. It's the important and difficult choices that leave us confused and uncomfortable about who we are and the choices we've made to support that person we desire to be. At these times, we need to have practiced how to make a choice. We need to know who and what we desire to be, so difficult and sometimes painful choices lead to truthful and satisfying experiences. When we look back and see the choices we've made have given us self worth, we can smile and continue on to more experiences, with no regrets for who we are. Our characters are not for others to judge. We judge our character ourselves, if worthy of existence.

The most advantageous aspect of experience is its ability to produce habits based in a truth. Many professionals or experts, in a given subject, will explain their expertise comes more from the experience of previously dealing with a given situation than anything else. This is particularly true where a quick response to a situation is required.

To react from habit is much quicker and easier than having to consciously consider and contrive a response. It leaves our resources free to deal with more difficult or ensuing aspects. However, understand these useful habits are derived from trained, truthful experience, not reactions to stimuli.

CHAPTER SEVEN

HAPPINESS

Happiness is a very elusive idea. It has a wide possibility of definitions, yet few truly know what happiness really is. I like to define happiness as waking up each morning with a smile on my face. However, even though I consider myself happy, I still wake up grumpy and need a shower before I'm reasonable again.

What I mean by waking up happy is that each day I enjoy my life and see beauty in the world, no matter what experience passes my way. I do this by putting life in perspective. If I'm healthy and have another day to make things better or to just enjoy, I truly have no complaints. Everything else I've chosen or been forced to deal with by my existence is just the reason for living or existing at all.

I observe life as though it cannot be perfect or there would be no reason for the human existence at all. Our existence takes place on the premise we need to have something to do or accomplish. Otherwise, why would we exist at all?

Creation, the act of being creative and manifesting it, is the highest accomplishment of existence there can ever be. With each day, I'm able to create the idea I am happy.

However, if this defines happiness, just explaining happiness doesn't allow others to know how to come to this point. It doesn't provide a definition that allows others to know they're at a point of possible happiness. If we can't pinpoint some basis for a definition of happiness, how do we surrender to the understanding of whether or not we're happy? If the definition of happiness is transient, can we not allow our confidence in our understanding that we're happy to change, even though we've not changed?

This is like a landlord telling you your rent changes every month. You never know what to expect. Sometimes the rent is a good amount, sometimes it's a bad amount. Even though the place you rent doesn't change, the definition of its worth does.

Having a definite definition for what happiness is for you is the only way to determine, without doubts, that happiness is or can be achieved by you. Fortunately, there is a formula for happiness. Even if this formula is fulfilled for us, unless we're willing to recognize it and accept it, it may not bring us happiness. Knowing the formula is as important as achieving the acceptance of happiness. The formula is rather simple and consists of two parts.

Survival, which consists of the elements of air, water, food, clothing, shelter and health, is one part. Sufficient love is the second part.

I know this may seem a simple definition for happiness and many won't want to agree with it. Let's take a closer look at the formula.

First, look at the survival part. If we're not able to survive, very little else matters. Our ancestor's lives were consumed more and more with survival, the further back in time we go. Thousands of years ago, it was the production of food, war and disease that consumed much of human existence. Going further back, just finding enough food was often the entire focus of existence.

Air is an obvious survival need. If we didn't have enough air to breath, it would be a very unpleasant world and I'm sure we all agree we'd do just about anything to get air. Survival is the first need to acquiring a state of happiness. Once happiness is attained and recognized, some parts of survival may become less critical. If we're worried about the staples of maintaining life, we have little time or patience for other things in our lives. Although I'm trying to provide a guide for happiness that isn't monetary based and can be achieved for most successful individuals, there's no doubt that having sufficient money or monetary means can provide for your survival. In this view, yes, money can help acquire happiness.

Air, food and water are obvious parts of the survival equation. Clothing and shelter are the protections from nature, which allow us to relax and begin to contemplate other aspects of existence. If we're constantly worried about freezing to death, being eaten by predators or baking in the sun, our minds stay alert to dangers and protection, instead of relaxing and enjoying life. However, as leisure time becomes available to the mind, it allows the intellect to imagine and create, either through desire or necessity.

Physical and mental health are necessary elements of survival. If your physical health is at risk, it obviously has the possibility of distracting our lives and we concentrate on feeling and being in better health. If our mental state isn't healthy, we may never have the ability to recognize the difference between simply surviving and living a happy life.

When survival needs are met, the intellect can relax, giving the soul the opportunity to be heard. The soul begins to express the desire to understand, invent, accomplish and experience new possibilities, beyond current understandings. This is the new frontier for mankind, this expression of desire, and has created new issues as well. As is true for all parts of this universe, there are laws in which the human desire must be based and which we are unable to circumvent. We can, however, understand and manipulate these laws, based on their character. This is where the element of love becomes important.

A sufficient quantity of love, I have observed, is the second element of existence that is necessary for the human experience, in order for a person to be happy. I have also observed that, given enough parameters, a person will deny any other desire, except survival, in order to experience the love they desire.

Provide an individual any other element of life and deny one element in the equation for happiness and you'll discover the person is still searching to be happy. Give the same person all the elements in the equation for happiness and they can live without other things they may feel are of great importance and still be happy.

If you're willing to accept a definition, at least some definition, of happiness, you have some way of determining whether or not you're happy. Without a solid definition for happiness, we are left confused by any answers we provide. Truth and knowledge regarding a definition of happiness allows us to provide an answer without confusion. Knowing you are happy allows you to be happy. Knowing you are not happy allows you to accept that you need to make confident choices that result in confident efforts to become happy.

This is the basis for happiness. Being willing to accept it is the only path to true happiness. Acquiring sufficient love, and the peace and joy we all desire from love and loving relations, is the challenge most of modern civilization is dealing with, in order to be happy. Expertise in how to become wealthy, be a number one contender in some specific occupation or activity or provide the survival needs for your life is not the subject in need of clarification. Documentation on such subjects is prolific and readily available. Good techniques and education in opening our hearts and souls to our desires, including the desire for a sufficient amount of love, are what my observations show we need.

CHAPTER EIGHT

THE HUMAN EXPERIENCE

THE HUMAN EXPERIENCE IS made up of many components. Why it exists and what reasons there may be for our existence are questions to which I don't expect to find answers to in this lifetime. Rather than demanding answers, I spend my life dealing with the issues of life I can influence. That we do exist, that we are here in this existence and going through this experience, is really all we have.

Philosophical postulation about all the possibilities beyond our existence in this life is an interesting prospect, but the willingness to buy into a life based in little factual information, in order to feel complete as a person, truthfully lacks. Time before me and after me is a mystery that allows for playful pondering of possibilities, but makes no real contribution to the here and now. If the before and after is all we're here for, why be here at all?

Our experience is full of tangible issues, survival, emotion, vision, touch, smell, noise, creativity, invention, exploration and discovery. If we believe in reasons, there must be reasons for the things we can experience here and now. I've observed that the way we choose to mentally accept that which is real and around us helps us enjoy more of the human experience. Something as simple as changing the way we say something, which leads to how we perceive something, can help in guiding us down a path of greater enjoyment.

We have many degrees of perception. We like or dislike someone or something. We love, we hate or we're indifferent. Imagine this: If we never hated anything, this would lead us to a life of finding either joy or indifference in all that is. If we used worlds like, "I like it the least," we could train our minds to not hate.

Many peoples and tribes around the world don't have words for things they don't experience, which leads me to believe many things we experience we do through choice, rather than necessity. If these tribes can live without the ability to express a given experience, they must never truly experience it.

Do we truly hate things or can we live without this experience and eliminate the word that allows us the choice to live this experience? Just to know we prefer one thing over another and to choose that which we prefer, rather than deny and hate the other choice, can produce a more joyful experience of life. Opening our souls to the knowledge that all the experiences of life, even the painful ones, are part of the beauty of life is a choice over seeing the opposite.

We choose how we'll experience most things in the mental and spiritual existence. We only think, through false education, that we're victims of mental and spiritual law. In truth, the law of the spirit and mind is impersonal, as are all universal laws. If we truthfully understand it, we can use it to our advantage. We are only victims of false information, confusion and how we choose to experience this life.

One of the laws of intellect is that we can choose. "The Law of Choice", which was created by the "Law of Free Will." We have control over how to make choices for what we want. We have control over making choices about how we want to experience something. We choose how we let stimulus affect us and how we choose to react to stimulus.

The more of life I'm willing to love, the more love there is in my life. Choosing to make choices based on seeing life as an adventure, something to be explored and discovered for its wonders is all it takes to improve a bad situation. Even if you're deluding yourself about a bad situation being good, it still works, although not being truthful about our situations usually causes negative consequences. However, you can choose to not allow a bad situation to be the end of all other good things in your life. You can choose to not let it take control over your choices about how to experience the world or the moment.

These choices are always in your control, due to the Law of Choice. We can choose how to experience life.

The less of life I find ugly, the less ugliness there is in my life. This may sound too simple to be true, yet it is truth. By simply selecting and choosing the way I let something affect me, I can experience my existence in a more desired manner. The self-evident truth in these statements is hard to refute. Sure, it's hard to find beauty when feeling pain, in the crimes of man, in physical handicaps, in world disasters that can torture and take loved ones from us, in children without parents or with disease or birth defects.

We can look at the horror in such things or we can try to find reasons for such things that can produce beauty, or at least truth, so we're not confused by such pain. Feeling pain is a natural part of existence. Coming to an understanding about painful situations is the only way to overcome the despair that often accompanies pain. I've found the willingness to accept Free Will for what it is and has to be, in order to exist at all, brings me to an understanding that allows me to see why life's horrors are just a part of life, leaving me the ability to see all of life as a beautiful thing.

If there were no bad, we would have nothing to compare to good. Without suffering, there would be no reason to try to be better. If there is not reason to overcome, to change things, life becomes only existence, not an experience. The more awful we can be, the greater the idea of good can be. The larger the gap between two opposing poles, the greater the distance to be compared.

This is not meant to advocate being a tyrant. Most tyrants die young. This is an observation. Recognize that if you are fed, clothed and have a roof over your head, you have room in your life to begin looking for the beauty in life and leaving the hatred behind.

What I want to convey in this book is that life must be experienced. We will feel, even when life is as good as we can imagine it. Our bodies react to physical and emotional experiences. There's no way out of this, except death. No amount of focus on who and what we are, on living in principle, can provide a safe haven from the experience of being a human being. However, through recognition of the truthful realities of our universe, which relate to the existence of our spirit, we can discover and use the Laws of our universe to produce, understand, choose and create a more desired experience and existence. Having found, through education and observation, more realistic purposes for my emotions, free will and senses, I'm able to live my most truthful desires.

There is a saying, "The boy with the most toys wins." I believe, instead, "The boy who goes through the most toys wins." I'd rather experience life than collect it. Realizing and living the experiences you desire is true success. Manifesting the experiences others want you to believe is what you want is the blind leading the blind.

No desire, thought, wish, dream or idea means anything, without an effort to make them real. Again, manifesting your life, the one you desire for yourself, is the ultimate success.

As we attain and experience our desires, we become content with our existence. I'm not referring so much to the material desires, but more the experiences of our connections with this universe and its inhabitants. When you are loved by those with whom you interact, it becomes a wonderful life, regardless of how much money or how many material possessions you obtain.

If you were given all the material possession you could ever want, but told you could never experience love of any type, not even love of your possessions, would you want to pay that price? Would you choose to never know what it's like to love or be loved? I hope you've experienced the connection of love, or possible love, at least once, for some small moment in your life.

The example of your ability to attract your deepest desires becomes a light for others to follow. I've observed this light is very attractive to others. Your peace with your existence allows you to become a mentor for others, helping them to find the happiness and joy they've always thought should be possible.

Many spiritual disciplines teach that the spirit is the way to fulfillment and that giving up material possessions is either the only way or the most effective way to obtain enlightenment. I've observed otherwise. While material possessions can easily get in the way of the truth of our desires, they are just another part of existence, once survival is assured. Such possessions do have the ability to produce joy, if they are understood and experienced from the truthful point of view that they aren't necessary for happiness. Denial is denial. Denial of our desires, particularly when we know we have the ability to obtain them, only breeds discontentment and resentment.

The experiences you crave in your life are possible, once you admit that your desires are real and important and understand you are the one with the power to make the choices which will make the experiences you wish to enjoy in this existence possible. Remember, only death relieves you of the aspects and responsibilities of your human experience. Our ability to be infinitely creative is beautiful, if you're willing to accept the responsibility for your existence. If your existence isn't as you wish, it's not your parents' fault or your wife's fault or even society's fault. It is your fault, if you don't choose to be whom you want to be.

CHAPTER NINE

WHO ARE WE?

F INDING OUT WHO WE are and what we want to be is the key
to eliminating confusion in our lives. Eliminating confusion
brings the most inner peace I've ever observed or experienced.
It may seem a simple statement. "Finding out who you are
and what you want to be will help you live a more happy and fulfilled life." But I've found it's not as simple as it seems. Most people
I talk with cannot articulate who they are or what they want to be.
As a result, they're unable to live their lives by making choices based
on a definition of what's best for them. Instead, they make choices
motivated by sources that have not and do not provide an observable truth that their definitions for how to live life produce desirable
experiences.

Who are you? Not what do you do to make a living and survive
or what your name is, but who are you as a definable individual? A
simple way to explain this concept is to examine the roles you play
in your life. Are you a son or daughter, mother or father, wife or
husband, brother or sister? Are you a provider, a lover, a musician,
volunteer or even just a person?

What you are is as important as who you are. What you are is
the type of person you are in whatever role(s) you play. Are you an
available brother or sister, a loving spouse, a fair boss?

Whom and what we are cannot always be chosen, although
choices are still part of us. Whom and what we are can only be true
through the manifestation of our choices. If I desire to be a trustworthy spouse, but I choose to lie and cheat on my partner, I am not a
trustworthy spouse.

Knowing who and what we are is a personal attribute. It's important to no one but ourselves. Sharing this information with others is only important when we decide to communicate expectation of our lives with someone. Who you want to be and how you want to be is what makes you happy. The dreams we have for our lives, those we hold to be true in our souls and often daydream about, are the key to our state of being. Achieving the understanding that our most inner desires can be experienced is the ultimate joy.

Surrendering to a false proclamation that our desires are only unattainable myths is the ultimate failure. To fail at times, in trying to achieve our desires, is only part of the experience of living our lives. Accepting that our desires are unattainable fantasies is the only true failure of existence. I can profess I have experienced and observed that the dream is possible, but you must first understand what your true dream is.

Figuring this out and then finding what choices can and will produce these desires is a tool I learned from Stephen Covey's book, Seven Habits for Highly Effective People. Finding out who I was and what I wanted to be opened me up to understanding how to make choices that serve me best. I may still make a choice that's not good for me, but I tend to recognize that and am willing to take responsibility for the consequences. This leaves me with no need to lay my faults on someone else, especially someone important to me. It leaves me with no confusion about my choices. I no longer waste energy, time or effort, pondering the needs to justify my choices, beneficial or detrimental, for achieving my desired experiences, to myself or to others.

I've seen little that teaches us how to deal with the issues of confusion and doubt that cloud our happiness when we make choices. An experience that shows us how to open our minds and listen to what our heart and soul is telling us we need to be in order to be happy is an experience that very few of us have experienced. This type of experience can come in different forms. The lucky few who do experience how to let their minds serve their souls often have no idea what they've gained. However, their outlooks on life are often set into an understanding that allows them to make choices that manifest their desires.

Most of us didn't get the winning lottery spin that allows us to fall into a lucky understanding for happiness. The few who did get lucky are only victims of a condition they really know nothing about, but which produced a positive result for them. For me, I'd happily take the accident of the lucky situation, but I'd prefer the knowledge of understanding how and why.

Determining what your soul craves and what will enable you to lead a happier life is a simple process. It's all about finding out how you want to be remembered. As Mr. Covey said, "Begin with the end."

How do you want to be remembered? Who and what do you want people to recall? The answer to this is the key to making the choices that satisfy your soul. Most projects, all monumental and successful projects, start with the end in mind. You envision the finished product and then take the steps to achieve it. A building, a bridge or a house all begins with the concept of the finished product. So should we. We need to consider how we want to be remembered and then make the choices that allow us to achieve this conceptual person.

How can making choices that lead you to becoming your desired person make you happy? First, it gives you peace of mind, allowing you to rest your efforts to justify your decisions to yourself or others. This is true whether the need to justify your existence comes because you want to look good to others or are just confused, yourself, over your decisions.

You no longer have to deal with the confusion of whether or not a choice is best for you, whether a choice is beneficial or detrimental to becoming the person you desire to be.

Happiness is achieving, or heading in the direction of achieving, what your soul desires, being who and what you want to be.

The first step is to find out who you are. Are we building a bridge, a building or a house? We are the roles we are and have chosen to be. Some roles just are. We are born into the role of child, son or daughter. Even if our parents are deceased, we are still some sorts of child. If we have brothers and/or sisters, we are a sibling. Other roles we've chosen, such as being a musician or an athlete. Some things we may not have chosen from conscious decisions, such as that of student.

Sit down and write out who you are. Younger people will have fewer roles. As we get older, we tend to take on a few more roles. Keep your roles condensed, between five and ten for most of us. I find provider, spouse, lover, friend, person, student, professional, business man, athlete, artist, musician and such terms work well. There are various definitions for roles that suit each individual best, but keeping the roles generalized keeps the list from getting too long and hard to work with.

Yes, take the time to sit down and write this out. I've observed that documenting who you are and what you want to be is the one physical exercise that is necessary, in order to live a more accomplished and desired existence that I am trying to explain. The rest of the labor is the mental courage and mental thought processes to make and manifest the choices that will produce the type of person you want to be.

Now you have a list of who you are. The next step is to determine who and what you want to be. Again, this is a simple process.

Imagine you've passed away. You've died. Your life has ended. You have no more opportunities to change, to do, to accomplish. Imagine every person who has meant anything to you in your life, the good and the bad. Everyone you've known or come across is attending your funeral. Each one has a moment to speak in eulogy of your life, as they experienced you.

Imagine what it is you want to hear them say about you and what you want all these people with whom you've become familiar to hear about you. The memory of the person you've been. A truthful summation of your life. It has nothing to do with material items, which have no ability to reason, judge or care. The one thing you can take with you, the one thing that lives forever, is what you've truthfully been in your life and can be proven through how you are remembered.

Do this for each role you've listed. Write down the words that describe what you want to hear others say about you. What you want your spouse to say about the type of wife or husband you were. What you want your friends to say about the type of friend you were. This is what your soul desires from this existence. This is the person you want to be. This is an important revelation, worth repeating.

THIS IS WHAT YOUR SOUL DESIRES FROM THIS EXISTENCE, TO BE AND EXPERIENCE BEING THIS PERSON.

This may, at first, sound like you want to look good to others, in order to be who you want to be. However, you are not considering what they think you need to be. You're considering what it is you want to be, what you want to hear the world confess about you and what you want others to have experienced from you. You're not asking what others want from you. You're asking what you want for yourself.

It's not important whether you've been able to produce these ideals for yourself at this time. What's important is that you've defined what you want to be at the end of your life and this is the key to making decisions in your life now. Using this, look at the description for each role in your life. If you're a father, what kind of father do you want to be? Do you want to be kind, loving, patient, providing?

These ideas and ideals of who you want to be are principles. Living your life according to these principles, making choices based on principles, is character. Whatever influence you use to make choices in your life is your character.

Mr. Covey defines the influences used to make choices as "your center for living." Not only does living a life based on character built from principle make you proud of whom you are and provide self-worth, it also puts every decision you may need to make in much clearer understanding.

Whenever you feel uncomfortable about a situation, angry, sad or frustrated, test to see if you're being the person you want to be in the situation. Live in the moment. Lose all that you've been taught about what will make you happy and see if you're being the person you want to be. If you aren't, which is usually the case, alter the situation to what you desire it to be. If you are being who you wish to be, you can find peace in knowing you're living up to the principles of your life. Although it may be difficult to stand in that place at times, the questioning or the confusion regarding the best choices to make for yourself will no longer haunt you.

It takes courage to live a life based in principles and it doesn't eliminate the pains of life's journey. Some of the choices that are best for us aren't easy ones to make. At times, it can seem they're not producing what we desire for our existence. However, often the difficult choices are the ones that keep us on the path to our desires.

The knowledge that you are making a difficult choice, but a choice helping you become who you want to be, won't leave you with the doubts that have the ability to tear at your confidence. Instead, it allows you one more experience of self worth, which nothing can take away from you. This self worth has the ability to eliminate difficult times and issues in your life. It builds the foundation, which allows us to stop worrying about everyone else's judgments of our lives, judgments that most of time don't make any sense, when related to the existence we desire to experience for ourselves. It provides a life of choices that make it possible to experience the things you desire. But these principles must be based in truth.

Your principles must be based in truth about what you desire to be. Without this truth, we often limit our existence to what others think we should be. I desire much more than what most people have told me is possible. I have, in many areas of my life, achieved the dreams I felt were possible all my life, despite what others said.

I've accomplished this by making choices that make me what I want to be.

Using who we want to be as the basis for the principles of our character and using our character to guide us in making our choices may seem like a selfish way to live life. However, you will quickly see that many of the principles of your character will include desires beyond our individual existence. I have yet to observe anyone who purposely wants to be remembered as a selfish tyrant. These types of defined existence usually come from an unexamined and accidentally lived life.

Do you think Hitler wanted to be remembered as the leader of the holocaust? My observations indicate Hitler made choices based on fear, which came from being confused about how to achieve an idealistic, although unexamined and misguided, campaign. This is another controversial analogy. I have no idea if Hitler had greater issues of mental illness, which made him who he was. I'm just trying to make a point about choices, not a political point of view or possibility.

The point is, in order to keep on course in becoming who we desire to be, we need to have an idea of who we want to be. This includes the way we treat others, as well as the greater goals for humanity. Being humans, we'll often make mistakes in our behaviors, doing things we don't desire. However, having an idea of the direction we must travel to achieve our desires allows us to easily, confidently and quickly adjust our course, or behaviors, and get back on track.

Two books by Steven Covey, Seven Habits for Highly Effective People and Seven Habits for Highly Effective Families, explain in detail the aspects of principle based living and how the center for our lives can make it either more effective or difficult to make choices that produce the desired results. I highly recommend reading these books. I feel as if I've plagiarized Mr. Covey's work with my many references, but his teachings are only a piece of my observations. I couldn't explain my understandings without referencing his materials.

Choose your life, make choices based on who you want to be. Be a leader for happiness and happiness will seek you out, sometimes to excess.

Being what we want to be isn't specifically about what we do in life to survive or to fill our time. While understanding that these ideas can help us in all parts of our existence, I am referring to how we relate to ourselves and other people on a day-to-day basis. The way to a much happier life is choosing not to let others around us trigger responses that don't help us reach the goals of the existence we desire. While material security has its joys and pleasures, successfully surviving this existence is still not enough for us to be happy. Coping with everyday existence is what brings us our greatest confusion and stress. How to attain the love and personal experiences we desire is what leaves us confused and wanting.

I've observed that being and becoming the person you want to be is the path to happiness, through helping us acquire the amount of love we all desire. This, above all else, is the desired experience of our lives.

Accomplishments and creative expression are also desired, but if one is given the choice of one thing over another, our human souls need to experience soulful desires to be happy and only use other experiences to achieve the soulful desires.

CHAPTER TEN

COURAGE

L IVING LIFE, BASED ON your principles, and making choices that keep you true to those principles takes courage. No one said life, nor any of the issues I've been discussing, is easy. My observations have shown me most successful, happy and fulfilled humans are those who have courage. They are brave enough to take chances, to make the choices that are best for them, rather than choices that make them look good to others. These choices are usually what others feel you should do, in order to be happy and/or successful.

Courage means you have to be willing to give up what may be popular, in order to find your own happiness. Would you rather live, knowing you avoided a possible painful death that would have saved people you love, or die, knowing you're saving the people you love? Most of us will never face this type of life or death moralistic decision, but I use the extreme example to show that small choices we make ever day add up in our lives. How we will judge ourselves has the most influence on our existence. We can lie to others, but we always know the truth about ourselves.

Choosing not to better your life by hindering or destroying someone else's is often seen as weak. It's justified by being taught we might as well take all we can get, by any means, because that's what everyone is going to do.

Understand, being taught such ethically lacking principles isn't done consciously or from malicious motivation. The idea of being fair and kind to others is one I've observed as being a dominantly taught behavior. The fact is, many of the behaviors being taught in order to behave in an ethical manner toward others lack the ability to produce the desired results, because we're unable to question understandings. We've never been taught how to seek the truth, rather than just behaving as we're told to do.

Knowing the right choices for ourselves is not enough. We must take the risk and implement these choices. If the correct choice for me is to be kind to others, I must make the effort to be kind, rather than being cruel in order to look good and be acceptable to my friends and acquaintances. I must also have the courage to point out to others how poorly they're behaving, at least for my life, when they're being cruel.

It may seem I discuss the mentoring that occurs in our lives as though nothing good has or can come from it. This isn't what I mean to portray. Not everyone and everything is lying to us completely. I'm trying to show you that the smallest bit of untruth, in just the right or wrong place, can have a large negative affect on our existence.

Most mentors in our lives are kind and caring people, with nothing but good intentions, who often provide us with idealistic information to help us live our lives. Some, often much, of this information is positive and good for us. Most of the time it comes in the form of knowledge for survival. I am looking beyond survival, jobs, health and money. I'm addressing a higher desire for our existing, although I'm not excluding survival aspects in my observations.

It takes courage to provide a different possibility than that which is popular and reactive. It takes courage to be a light of truth and to lead, instead of following the same old clichéd life others regurgitate. However, people are attracted to light and you will find others who want and desire to be part of a truthful and courageous existence.

Simply believing and understanding who and what we want to be isn't enough. We must find the courage to act, in order to attain our desires. You cannot be a trustworthy person, if you don't speak the truth or if you fail to behave as you've said you would behave. Failing to keep promises and agreements makes you untrustworthy.

Of all the truths, keeping your word, keeping your promises and agreements, are the most powerful. Not keeping your word or acts of truth are potentially the most harmful.

You are how you behave. Desire is only a motivator. If we don't act on the choices we desire for our lives, we won't be what we desire. Te be a kind husband, I must do what it takes for my wife to see me as a kind person.

Decide who you are and what you want to be, make the choices that will lead you to be who you want to be and have the courage to make it happen. The achievement of our dreams is the ultimate proof of the success of our existence.

Courage is like any other aspect of life. Once practiced, it becomes easier to live by. Just like training to run a marathon, new habits take time to achieve. If you get up each day and decide to choose your path, rather than react from habit, each instance of conscious behavior will train your mind to behave from choices, not reactions. Train yourself to live life without the fear of being different. Train yourself to be who you want to be.

CHAPTER ELEVEN

LOOKING GOOD

L
ooking good. It's a primary message we receive from modern societies and the primary cause of confusion in our lives. From an early age, the first advice we receive is all about looking good to someone else. No advice about being happy, just looking good.

Growing up in Southern California, I was immersed in the physical aspects of looking good. Outer beauty catches our eyes, infatuates our desires and allows us to look special to others, if we have, or can attain, such beauty. If what we're told is to be believed, it allows us to go to college, make a good living and buy lots of special things, material things.

Looking good is the one unconscious desire that will make you extremely unhappy. It is the one subject that will make you fight against everything I've explained in this book. This learned desire, taught to us, not natural, leads us to conform to the desires of others. It dictates looking a certain way or behaving a certain way or believing in a certain way or thing, all based on what others think is important. We do this to be accepted and fit into the norms of our environment, defined by our ancestral history and based on what appears to work to produce a happy and successful existence.

Even if you believe you think for yourself and don't conform to others' expectations, there's a good chance you're doing this based on the need to look different, to look unique and self guiding, giving you some edge over others. You believe you look good by not being the same. This, in most cases, is just following a more minority path of conformity, as few choices in our lives are unique.

How do we stop the habit of trying to look good? We need only replace this behavior with the behavior of seeking the truth. Refuse to accept, to agree or disagree with, something you have no way of knowing is truthful. Even our opinions can be stated as just an opinion, therefore being based in truth.

If you have never experienced the subject or situation upon which you state an opinion, your ability to speak truthfully about the issue is greatly in question. If you have never tasted chocolate, you have no idea if you like it or not. Sure, deduction is possible, but deduction takes some knowledge, before it can bear much truth. Tasting raw cocoa is nothing like tasting milk chocolate, but tasting chocolate pudding is very similar to tasting chocolate pie.

Not seeking the truth and choosing to look good damages our happiness. One very common example is the relationship game. It's sad that the word, "game," comes up in something so important to our well-being as relationships.

I doubt many would argue with the idea that making a lover happy is something we want to do. Serving your spouse is often a very important and necessary part of committed relationships. Say your spouse expects you to be home at an expected hour, due to an already communicated agreement. Instead, you go out with some friends and when you get up to leave, to go home to the committed relationship in your life, you friends tease you about having to comply with what this special person in your life desires.

Do you look good to your friends, by proving you are your own person and can do as you please or do you admit the truth and realize you're not your own person and that meeting your commitment, which you wanted in the first place, is really what you desire? You can look good and make your so-called friends happy and upset your love or you can stand up for who you are and what you want and make the important person in your life feel happy and safe, served and honored. Going after what you really desire, truthfully desire, leads you to living the existence of your dream, not living a life to simply look good and court unhappiness.

Stop looking good and be happy. Often, the people we admire most in life behave in a manner that is best for them. We see them as leaders, not followers.

You will often find that what is truly best for you is often good for others as well. When we make choices that serve us, we begin to show others our true value, quality and character. You'll quickly find others are attracted to you, attracted to persons of desirable qualities. Life is much easier, when the world comes to you, to offer their resources and take part in your desires, rather than you having to go out and convince the world you have something of value to offer to be a part of it.

I've observed that the confidence, which comes from living a principle based life, is obvious to and of great interest to others and is the most attractive behavior to have. Having others want to be, in some way, a part of our existence is a huge accomplishment for our desires. It provides for joyful experiences that leave us assured of a happy existence and assured the choices we're making do produce desired results.

Chapter Twelve

PRINCIPLE BASED LIVING: CHARACTER VERSUS PERSONALITY

THERE'S BEEN A LOT of self-help guidance provided, based on traits of the human personality. Personality based guidance focuses on the way we represent ourselves. It contends that how we choose to outwardly exist can influence how we succeed in our efforts. Personality based help explains that if we just try harder, have a better attitude and are kinder to our surroundings, life can be more positive.

I'm going to be blunt. Changing our personality to fix our contentment with life is like putting a new coat of paint on a condemned building. It may look better, but it's still falling apart.

A personality has no way of eliminating confusion about our existence. Although it can produce more positive results for our efforts, it relies on defined behaviors, which we've been taught should produce the results we want. It doesn't address the confidence that comes from ourselves, when we are behaving in accordance with our desired character and defined principles.

This is not to say that working on your personality doesn't have positive benefits. The point is a shiny coat of paint doesn't remove rust. As long as you base your choices on how you look to others, how you affect others, you'll never be able to satisfy the never-ending list of expectation others will define for you. Their expectations will require you to conform, in order for you to have, or in most cases appear to have, the peace and confidence you've always dreamed of.

A character-based existence provides self worth no one can take away from you. I have never cheated on a committed intimate relationship. I admit I've behaved towards a friend in a manner I'm not proud of. Still, I can hold on to the behaviors I am proud of, no matter what happens in my life. These can never be denied, lost or taken away from me.

Your character is your confidence. This is true confidence, not confidence created in order to overshadow your doubts about your existence or who you are. It's a confidence that exists whether you're rich or poor, average or excellent, famous or normal. Confidence doesn't come from winning. It comes from knowing.

I know a number of people who have very pleasing personalities. However, some of them have lives that are in shambles, others I have no trust in and still others are very successful in business, but absolutely lost when it comes to love.

Character isn't just about being of high moral value and not taking advantage of others. It also affects the choices you make for the desired existence in all aspects of your life. A very kind and moralistic person, who selflessly helps others, can still fail in relationships of love, if their character is not based on principles.

If our choices on how to treat someone are based on how they treat us, no relationship will work. For example, every time a person is rude, you fuel the fires of discontent, if you treat them the same way. If you stay the course for who you want to be, you have no reason to let their mood affect your own, to feel negative about who you are or to fuel an already negative situation. You may find this situation has nothing to do with you and will pass by you as a little thing in your life, instead of something tragic.

If we depend only on our personality to get through situations by just being pleasant, we can still be confused by not understanding how the rudeness of others is really just their problem. Just because we don't let our personalities outwardly show how we react to something doesn't mean we're not dealing rudely to someone who's being rude to us. It only means we're not letting them see how we're dealing with a situation. We must know, within ourselves, that we are not treating someone rudely, nor do we desire to do so, just because that person is being rude. This fills us with the confidence it takes to know our behaviors are the best ones for our existence, which eliminates confusion about our choices.

When we influence our choices about the type of person we want to be, based on our desires to behave in a manner which will produce the experiences we wish to manifest, we eliminate the confusion of not really knowing if the choices we make are the best choices for our happiness. We have no reason to waste time or energy on doubtful thoughts and possible justifications for choices we're not sure are right. We no longer berate ourselves for ineffective choices that clutter our minds, which disrupt any possibility for peace or confidence for the direction in which we're guiding our existence.

I would much rather have a car that runs and performs like a Ferrari, but is in need of a good paint job, than a vehicle that looks nice, but runs poorly. Having a great running vehicle that looks good is the ideal, of course. Living your life, through knowing your desires and basing your life in principles, is important. Being respectful, gracious and pleasant has its rewards, too.

I know of no human being who doesn't have some sort of philosophy for living life. Something that serves as a center to which they cling, for meaning or purpose for what they're experiencing, and serves as a motivator and justification for how and why they exist.

If our philosophical center for how to exist and experience our lives is based on something that exists beyond our influence, we abandon responsibility for our lives and the choices we make. Motivation for our character, centered in sources other than our principles, allows us to blame these sources for success or failure. We don't have to take responsibility for our lives and choices, the achievement of our desires or the lack thereof.

The definitions for our character will be transient, because outside sources seldom agree or remain stable. Consistent terms for motivation change as well, depending on conditions beyond our control or influence. This produces another place for confusion, as happiness is never about making someone else happy. We won't make someone or something else happy by trying to live up to their standards. We can only be part of and experience someone else's happiness. We can easily imagine the possibility our own desires and desired experiences could be denied, if our chosen influences are defined by entities beyond our influence or control.

The soul is the mediator of our happiness. When the soul despairs, due to understanding it is not, may not, can not or will not achieve what it desires, it fails to be motivated or to motivate. The soul can despair, because of the feeling of failure to achieve desires. This is the ultimate in human failure and loss. The symptoms of a soul's despair manifest through many different characteristics, but the cause is always based in the confusion or despair of not knowing what choices to make to manifest at least the possibility of achieving what the soul desires.

As we learn the skills that clearly define the principles which have the ability to influence our choices and lead us to choices with the ability to manifest the person we desire to be, we gain confidence in our choices. While this may not necessarily change the effort it takes to make a difficult choice or the possible consequences of a choice, it places us in a position to use the best of our abilities in the process. It will be obvious, either before the choice is actually made or after it's been made, either consciously or by mistake, that this was or was not the best choice for us.

Eliminating confusion, through understanding how to make better choices, isn't always about making the best choice. It's about eliminating the internal struggle between the soul and the mind about which of these two entities is best able to be the guiding influence for choices that serve us best. Having the ability to determine when a choice was not an effective choice for our desires still eliminates the confusion normally produced when mentally pondering past choices. Clearness of mind is not about perfection. It's about clearly and confidently being able to distinguish an effective choice from a lesser or ineffective choice, whether the choice is before us or in the past.

Only through character-based guidance, based on a set of defined principles we desire to live by, can we have influences with the ability to guide us to make choices that will manifest an existence the soul desires to experience.

Real security in life comes only from one place, your character.

Basing our lives around principles doesn't mean we put religion, family, work or other subjects in second place. It means we live our lives through conscious choices. Many of us believe God comes first. God can still come first, if you live a life centered on principles.

This means you behave and make choices about the way you put God first in your life, centered on your principles, not on a church, religious leader, book or other influence that provides information or rules. You believe and obey religious rules and dogma you have chosen, if that choice represents your principles, and you're still living a life which is both Godly and principle based.

What we choose as most important in our lives should not be how to make a choice. The process of how to make choices is what we use, as a tool, to determine what is most important in our lives. How we make a choice is only a tool. What we put first in our lives comes from how we make our choices. Whether a choice is made conscientiously, habitually or reactive, how we make a choice will determine what we choose as important to our lives. So, I would suggest making your choices conscientiously if you want to experience that which is "most" desired and important to you.

The example of God being put first in our lives is only one of many possibilities of what anyone may want to believe should come first. Family, business, honor and country are but a few other possibilities. The point is, you must base your choices on your principles, not someone else's influential choices.

CHAPTER THIRTEEN

TRUST AND TRUSTWORTHY

T RUST IS THE ABILITY to believe in someone or something, without requiring proof. Trustworthy is having a character that makes others confident that what you confess is real and true. To lie or mislead others is not a trustworthy act.

To confidently and willingly serve, or surrender, one must know truth and must provide it in all aspects of his or her life. To serve, you must know and understand the truths about the person or service you're serving, if you're to provide what it requires. To surrender, you must trust that to which you're surrendering. Trust allows us to feel free of fear or doubts that close us off from or prevent our sharing of our inner truths, which allow us to experience the most sacred and personal parts of our being. If a white flag of surrender were shot at when waved, no one would trust surrender as a possibility.

Promises are a form of trust we ask others to have in us. Our word is all others can know of us. If we don't act in the manner we profess from our mouths, we cannot be trusted. Only the foolish, headed for confusion, put their trust in someone who lies, someone who doesn't keep his or her promises or fails to behave in a manner that honors his or her spoken proclamations.

The worst thing we can do to a person we love or care about is to break a promise. I'm not including physical abuse in this statement. I'm discussing situations in life that represent more normal, positive circumstances. Physical abuse of a loved one is a sickening abuse and should never be considered normal.

The common vows we share with someone within a marriage are the highest form of character someone can live up to. Once this promise is broken, trust is almost impossible to regain. It's possible to redefine the relationship and hold on to something that has possibilities of being of worth and value to us, but a return to the innocence that can make a dream come true is lost forever. Don't underestimate the power of your promises or your word. It can elevate when kept and destroy when broken or disrespected.

We are what our behavior shows. We may desire to be a certain type of person, but in order to be that person, we must behave as the person is defined, to truly become so. I may desire to be awful or evil, but if I behave with goodness and kindness, then I'm good and kind.

Few of us consider the power of our trust and honesty, when mentoring our children or any children. There are spiritual points of view, which explain a child's parent is perceived from the child's point of view as being God. Parents are seen as Omni by their children and have the power of mentoring a child's life with the smallest of choices. Trust from a child is almost unconditional, at least at first.

I've observed that consistency and honesty are the most powerful tools for raising a successful child. Consistency in behaving and acting as we say we will, leaves our children no reason to doubt how their parents will behave. Honesty is a powerful and positive tool for raising healthy, productive and happy children. They come to know we speak the truth and are willing to seek the truth from us. They have no doubts and have no fear we are consciously or unconsciously misleading them, which would give them little confidence in us.

A parent who misleads a child, no matter how small the deceit, produces a motivation for the child to consciously or unconsciously search for truth in other places and persons. As children grow and information provided to them by mentors, such as parents, is discovered to be either false or misleading, children will show signs of what is called rebellion, in order to search out a more accurate truth. They often end up testing possibilities for themselves, stumbling through life, making mistakes and creating scars that only leave them more confused about their existence.

Children look to us for the truth. When we lie to them, they seldom respect us as trustworthy mentors in their lives. This means any lie, even the innocent ones we find cute, in order to play out an enchanting experience. Think about it. If your child sees you as God, all knowing and all powerful, and accepts your guidance with no conditions, what damage is done to their trust, when they discover you're lying to or misleading them, even if it seems cute or innocent? We can promote creativity through imagination, without having to mislead or lie to our children.

I do my best to never lie to my children. Being human, I often tell my children I'm not prepared to discuss something with them, when I find myself flustered about a question. I can take some time to figure out how to explain the truth to them or I can explain this isn't the correct time in their lives to discuss a particular subject.

I love my children. I never want them to have any reason to not trust me to do my best to provide them with the truth about our existence. I want them to have as little confusion as possible, regarding what it will take for them to find happiness, and to know where to go to get honesty in their existence.

Chapter Fourteen

POINT OF VIEW

THROUGHOUT THE ENTIRE UNIVERSE, no two people or things have the exact same point of view. This is physics, as we understand it today. No two things or pieces of matter can exist in the same place at the same time. Therefore, no two things or people can have the same point of view at the same given moment, unless one wants to explore the concept of "Black Holes," which is another subject and not applicable here. Throughout this book, I'm trying to explain my point of view and, at the same time, guide you to also consider a point of view I've had the pleasure of experiencing.

The "Law of Perception" is generated from our singularity within the relativity of our universe. We can only see, experience or perceive our universe from our individual point of view. Other sources may explain another point of view to us, but we can only experience a single point of view at first hand.

Why is this important? It has to do with learning from other aspects, other points of view. Other people see the universe differently than you do or than I do. Others may see it very closely or similarly to the way we see it, but it's impossible for any two of us to see existence exactly the same way. This is the most accurate definition of uniqueness. If we cannot be unique, why is there an existence of more than one? This uniqueness and point of view partially explains why truths are important. Someone else may observe the same situation you do, yet experience it differently and explain it differently. This doesn't mean either one of you isn't being truthful.

When I look at an object from one side, or one point of view, and someone else looks at the same object from the other side, a different point of view, we may explain it as appearing to have very different aspects and characteristics. Yet, each is being completely truthful about what is being observed.

This is particularly important to remember when we study or read about subjects of interest, particularly information from the past. We need to understand the point of view from which it was originally observed or the point of view at the time it was explained and documented.

A point of view can be a physical place, a date in time, a mental or emotional or spiritual basis or any combination of elements. For example, when reading the Bible, one needs to understand the point of view from which it was written or it will seem as though the piece of knowledge being experienced is quite archaic and has no merit today. However, if you read it from the point of view of the time period and references involved, it has valuable information. Using this approach, look to the messages it's trying to explain, which are simply on how to live a full and complete life. Using the proper point of view, you'll learn many positives ways to be happy.

Let's look at point of view from the angle of generations. Our parents were born a long way from where we were born. Our point of view of our universe is much different from that of our parents, twenty or more years prior to our birth, due to our differing positions in the cosmos at the times of our births. If you calculate the spinning of the world, the orbiting of the sun, the sun orbiting the galaxy and the galaxy moving in the universe, our parents' point of view of the universe on the day they were born is much different than ours.

To say astrology has some impact on how we perceive things would have some truth. The universe is in a given position and matrix at any given time and is different for each individual. This is calculable. This allows us to have some understanding of how other individuals may see the universe and gives us some factual data to help us understand their point of view. I am neither advocating nor negating astrology. This is just a good way of showing it's possible to gather data that can be used to determine why someone may see things quite differently, yet truthfully.

Understanding does not come from a closed mind. Knowing we see very little of our entire universe and exploring other points of view can provide us with a greater and more truthful understanding, which allows us to ask questions and seek further knowledge, rather than being arrogant and behaving as though we know it all and have nothing more to learn.

Chapter Fifteen

POINT OF VIEW AND RELATIONSHIPS

LOVE AND LOVING RELATIONSHIPS are one of the highest of the soul's desires. Their attainment is one of the keys for an existence of experiences we desire. There is a close relationship between understanding points of view and understanding and experiencing relationships.

I love to use controversial examples. They tend to make a point more clearly than a safe, generic example.

One Judea-Christian commandment is to not commit adultery. First, we have to define the word adultery, which has been translated from other languages and passed down through thousands of years. For this example, let's stick with the definition that adultery means having sex outside of an existing marriage. Let's define marriage as a committed, monogamous relationship.

Committing adultery breaks the promises made regarding that relationship and shames and hurts the others involved. This is the normal consequence of the situation. This takes place without truthful relations. It's usually done in secret from someone who is part of that marriage and it breaks the promise of forsaking all others. I believe possibilities exist beyond this understanding, but with this example I'm not trying to deal with the anomalies of life, I'm dealing more with the commonalities. The act of breaking a promise of commitment produces confusion and often result in pain, or worse, for someone. I think this is a simple understanding of the commandment.

Having sexual relations with a married person to whom you are not married is just as relevant today as it was four thousand years ago.

Let's look at the more controversial aspect, not having sex before marriage. The King James Bible, I Corinthians 7:2, "Nevertheless, to avoid fornication, let every man have his own wife and every woman have her own husband". Most religious organizations have, or provide, little evidence for the reasoning behind this rule other than it is written, so you must obey. This is a ludicrous way to look at things and to convince anyone of the need to abstain from an apparent pleasure. It's also not a very intelligent way to see the truth, accepting it just because I read it or someone told me this was the rule. Personally, I'd like to observe, or at least be informed of, some positive results of such a rule, in order to see the truth in its purpose.

Let's look at this rule from two points of view. First, thousands of years ago, the consequences of sexual activity before marriage could have many negative and difficult consequences. Although they would have been important, I'm going to leave out cultural or social issues, because those involve making choices on looking good to others, which we've agreed is not a good basis for choices.

One major consequence of premarital sex was getting pregnant and being able to provide for and mentor a child. Another was the control of sexual diseases. Another was the maturity to make sex enjoyable. Many of these reasons are no longer a large concern in today's society, due to advancements in knowledge. Birth control, doctors and education are all available to us today, to control and alleviate these concerns.

There are, however, still good reasons for abstaining from premarital sex today, reasons that also had merit four thousand years ago. Sexual relations before marriage can, and most often do, produce a false understanding and disastrous expectations of committed monogamous relations.

Men want sex, but they also want to feel unique, loved and important to someone. The surrender of a woman to a man is the most intoxicating experience he will ever know. It makes a man feel special and loved. It makes his uniqueness special in the world.

The deepest surrender a woman can give is to allow a man to enter her and take on the consequence of possibly having his child. She surrenders to the pleasure she may receive from him, without convicting him of faults and mistakes in his behavior. A woman's sexuality attracts special attention from a man.

This is the natural way of our existence. However, we must remember we exist with the ability to affect our natures in many different ways. We are no longer just part of nature. We are influential to nature, both on purpose and by accident.

Women desire to feel safe and secure, cared for and served, unique and loved. The special feeling a man can give a woman, when he's courting her, is what her dreams, her heart and soul, have been telling her should be real. She is looking for a man who takes the effort to get to know her, considers her desires and needs above his, to show her she is of worth to him. His efforts, displays of affection, desires to keep her safe and take care of her satisfy the desires she wishes to experience, physically, emotionally and intellectually. Any observant male is well aware of this and knows how to court a woman he desires, whether for marriage or for sexual experiences.

Some women desire sex for physical satisfaction, some for the gift of giving, some for the goals it can achieve. Regardless of reason, if a woman doesn't feel taken care of and served by her suitor, she will cease to desire sex from him.

I am assured, from my observations, that in most cases, neither gender does any of this courting just for the purpose of having sex. With few exceptions, most who boast of wanting sex and nothing more are just trying to protect themselves from possible pain and/or looking bad to others.

There are those who know exactly how to use their abilities to get instant satisfaction. I've not observed that this produces desired experiences. More often than not, someone gets hurt in these types of situations. Most of us are looking for the dream of true romance and being of enough unique quality to have someone want to make a life long commitment to us. Even if we don't desire to accept that commitment, it's fulfilling to be the receiver of this type of affection.

The sad truth is most relations move quickly into sexual experiences, long before we ever get to really know the truth about who someone is. Short-term rewards from sexual satisfaction can, and are, easily used as motivation for coaxing desires for commitment. Sex can be used as a gauge to determine the quality of the relationship or as a tool to manipulate a relationship, even when we have no desire to allow such behaviors in our experience.

Relationships founded in sexuality, particularly where sex is part of the relationship early on, lack the basis of true love. Such relationships are built on the giving and receiving of physical satisfaction. Men feel they've found the woman of their dreams and the sexual gratification they receive in the beginning is the way the relationship will continue. Women feel that all the nice things the man is doing and his attentiveness to her needs and desires represent whom he is and how he's going to act over the long term of the relationship.

As time goes by and life's realities set in, the man becomes less attentive, assuming he's paid the price for what he deserves from his mate. The woman, still wanting to feel special and not just a sex object, begins to test the male's motivations for loving her, coaxing desired activities or behaviors that show he loves her for something other than her sexual favors. She often has no understanding of what's happening or why she's behaving as she is.

A snowball of negative behaviors and feelings becomes part of the relationship. The man wants the same sexual activity and participation the woman provided at the beginning of the relationship. The woman begins to hold back sexual participation, testing to see if she's loved for herself. The more the woman holds back from intimate sexual activity, the more the man pressures and demands it. The man begins to feel unloved, because he's not receiving the gift he first fell in love with, and the woman feels used only for her body.

It is only natural for people to fall into comfort zones. It's equally natural that life's realities will cause friction and there will be a slow down of lustful romance and efforts put into intimate relationships over the long term. Nonetheless, the desire and ability for sexual intimacy in a relationship built on loving the person, rather than only sexual intimacy, will create an increase in sexual satisfaction. Each has the assurance that sex isn't necessary in order to feel loved, and the deepening desire to satisfy his or her lover's desires produces a relationship that becomes more intimate and desirable. Each benefit from the growth of something they're experiencing, which is what they've always believed should exist.

Let's go back to the point of seeing things from a given point of view. While many reasons given for abstaining from sexual activity before a commitment have little merit today, the primary reason for allowing or hindering intimate growth between two people is as important now as it was thousands of years ago.

Taking time to discover that you truly care for and are attracted to someone, without sex, is the key to a long-term relationship. Allowing ourselves to look beyond today and see things from infinite possibilities and points of view allows us to see truth much more completely and comprehensively. Seeing the point of view, in which such a commandment as "Thou shalt not commit adultery" or the proclamation of "Nevertheless, to avoid fornication, let every man have his own wife and every woman have her own husband" was presented, allows us to look beyond our own justifications for not understanding or agreeing with these statements. It prevents our descending into the complete abandonment of such works as the Bible, works whose teachings can have merit in our lives'.

Good, long term relationships do not come from sex. Good, long term sex comes from good relationships.

CHAPTER SIXTEEN

LIVING IN THE MOMENT

"LIVING IN THE MOMENT," is a phrase used frequently in the New Age self-help area. What does it actually mean? Can it really help in any way or is it just another cliché to be used as a crutch for living life?

"Living in the moment," if understood properly, will have an affect upon achieving our desires.

Living in the moment means not using past experiences to shape the way we choose to view, experience or make choices about a current situation. It means not reacting to things in our lives by habit, but instead making each reaction a conscious choice.

I'm as guilty as anyone who argues that if we didn't use past events to help us with current situations, we could never learn to improve our lives or ourselves. We would be taken advantage of and could never protect ourselves from the great, big, dangerous world. Yes, I agree that, once you've burned yourself on a hot stove, it makes no sense to touch a hot stove again. There is merit to learning from past experiences. This begs the question, when do we use our past experiences and when do we live in the moment?

Let's restate the phrase. Instead of "living in the moment," let's use "live consciously." To live consciously is to treat each situation individually and to act from a conscious thought process, instead of acting through a subconscious reaction, a result of habitual, taught behavior. Use your intelligence and past experiences to consciously evaluate productive reactions to life's stimuli.

Habits don't allow us to get past difficulties in our lives, because we don't think about why we do something. We simply react. I've observed that people keep experiencing problems in their lives because they continue to react to life's stimuli, to situations and circumstances, in the same, habitual manner they've always used. This produces the same results they've gotten in the past.

I've also observed that living consciously is important to your quality of life. When we're told to live in the moment, we're being told to make a choice, based on information in front of us at that moment in time, qualified and combined with information we've gained from past experiences. We don't ignore these past experiences, but we don't let them control us unconsciously. We pause to think as mature, intelligent and rational beings, instead of simply reacting from habit. This is the key to living in the moment.

Unfortunately, we find it easier to react through habits than to analyze and consider our reaction, and then base it on information and truth. When stimulated to act – or more often, react – we need to stop for a moment and think over the situation. We need to stop reacting out of habits, based on past experiences or learned behavior.

Stopping to think about the best way to act or behave in a given situation is just the first step to living in the moment. In order to act in a manner which can build a happier existence for us, we must know how we wish to act, what choices we desire in our lives and then have the courage to make those choices. If we do this, what manifests from a stimulated incident is what we desire.

It's usually easier to think things through when life is good and we have the time to think. However, life's biggest issues and mistakes most often come when we're emotional and time is precious. This is when we let habit take over, take control. Most of us have habits that are not only against our best interest, but more often than not are based on false understanding.

If you talk with experts in any given field, you'll find that few believe natural talent produces an expert. It aids in the possibility of expertise, but the consensus is that repetition and practice make it possible to react to a situation in the most effective manner, because you've trained yourself to know what to do in a given situation. Train yourself with poor techniques and you'll produce poor results. Train yourself in effective techniques and you'll have a better chance of success.

How often have you trained yourself in what choices are best for you? Living in the moment will take practice. You need to retrain your thought process to use more effective techniques, seeking truth, knowing what you want and having the courage to be you.

Habits are difficult to change. By definition, habit means unconsciously doing something. It takes time and it takes effort to change habits to new choices and develop habits that produce your desires.

If we don't consciously recognize a behavior, we're not likely to have any idea there's anything we need to change. Habits will only change if you're willing to see them for what they really are, uncontrolled behaviors. Once you do that, you can change them to conscious behaviors. From truth, you can find behaviors that can produce your dreams.

CHAPTER SEVENTEEN

CHOICES AND HABITS

ONE THING WE ALL have in common is the ability to choose
how to experience life. The Law of Choice is a law of existence born from the Law of Free Will.

The word, "choice," is thrown around a lot these days. I can
understand how useless it may seem to tell someone in a bad situation they have choices they can make that will help them. It's easy to
proclaim the world has victimized us into our current situations and
we have no control over what's going on in our lives.

Let me be clear. The word choice means an alternative to one
thing or another. Choice is more about how we decide to experience
existence than about what flavor of ice cream we want. Choice is
about more than what school, profession, home, spouse or investment we select. Choice is accepting the truth about your current
situation and determining that if we're surviving and have love in our
lives, with tomorrow available to us to experience, there is a choice.
No matter what else is going on in our lives, positively or negatively,
we can choose how we let the way we perceive the situation affect our
experience. We choose whether or not to let things bother us. We can
choose whether or not we want something to bother us.

Most of us think how we experience things is out of our control. The truth is, it's our choice how we experience things. Reacting
from habit is a choice, especially after we've learned that reacting
from habit is something we do have control over.

I remember being at a point of despair in my life, when a friend
made the following pronouncement.

"I wish you the courage and strength to see how our choices
affect our experiences."

I admitted I knew I'd not always made the best choices for what I want in my life. He said that was one way to look at his statement, but it wasn't really what he meant. I wasn't sure what he meant, so I asked him to be blunt and just tell me exactly what he was trying to convey.

Before he could respond, understanding came to me. He meant that we choose how we want things to affect us.

I looked at the truth of my position and found I wasn't in such a bad place at all. I had the choice of how to be affected by my situation. As a result, I chose to participate in experiences that would allow me to enjoy that time in my life.

If someone walks by me on the street and calls me an idiot, I'll most likely brush it off and not care. I've made a choice that who and what that person is has no real importance in my life. On the other hand, if someone close to me in my life says the same thing, I may have a much more personal reaction. The choice I make here is that this person's opinion of me has some importance to me. Still, it's a choice I make, no matter how something makes me feel or react.

That said, no matter how important someone's opinion is to me, I should always rely on my own character for determining who I am. When I make the choice to do this, I leave out so many confusing issues other people produce, when giving opinions of me. This allows me much more peace and happiness. Rather than accepting the world's choices, which truly have no way of affecting me, I choose to let such stimuli be the responsibility of and owned by the source of the stimuli.

Making a choice to live my life, based on my principles, instead of based on outside influences, has eliminated a large amount of the confusion and pain that was once a part of my life. Choosing to seek truth in situations, including the truth I have choices on how to let things affect me, has led me to a happier existence.

Choosing the way I want to feel and who I want to be, rather than letting someone else produce reactions and feelings in me, lets me be in control of my existence. I gain power to influence the world around me. By not fueling fires that usually have nothing to do with the quality of who I am, I keep negative situations as small things in my life. This makes my existence more desirable, by allowing me more control over situations others define as out of their control, victimizing them as individuals.

Our habits, sometimes defined as our winning formulas, are often produced and retained from a very young age. Anger and temper tantrums are often habits we generated when we were just a few years old. If they worked for us back then, we continue to react to life, especially under stressful conditions, with the same behaviors. Just because they worked when we were young, doesn't mean they'll work for us as adults. We need to make efforts to recognize our winning formulas and try to stop reacting with the same old behaviors.

Test this for yourself. Watch others react to things in their lives. You'll see they often react with a few similar behaviors, which often get them into more trouble, rather than producing desired results or experiences.

Getting angry with someone we love, because of the way they're behaving towards others, or us, is a very common behavior. You'll notice it seldom produces a desired experience. Our anger over their behavior is not going to bring them to see the situation from our point of view.

Now, treat the situation differently. Think about whether the person's behavior has any true issue for you or not. Take no offense, even if taught, habitual behavior makes you think you should. Continue to behave as the person you want to be and you'll often find there's truly no issue at all. Usually, the other person will get over their temper tantrum and appreciate your ability to not fuel their habitual behavior.

Habitual behaviors seldom produce the results we desire. I cannot stress that enough. What we desire can be realized when we choose to behave in manners that produce the desired results.

If you feel the most important thing in your life is the quality of love in your life, make this more important than looking good to others. Make choices based on improving the quality of love in your life. Being loving, yourself, in situations not normally acceptable to society, often does this.

Most issues concerning the way we want things to be are, more often than not, tests for what we really desire. Most of what we do in life is done to find ways for qualifying the value for who we are. If we qualify who we are for ourselves, rather than depending on others' opinions, we stop having to produce tests and/or situations to prove our value to others. Value is knowing that our character is of a quality that cannot be questioned. This type of value, or self-assured and confident character, is attractive to the world in which we exist.

Choosing to be the person we desire to be is a choice we all can make. Choosing how we let things affect or experiences or feelings is a real and plausible option for our lives. Choosing to define our value in this world by truthfully evaluating whether we're living up to our own desired principles produces a confidence no one can take away from us. Living up to our own principles, instead of other peoples' desires and expectations, is living life in your desired character and is the best choice you can make, if you want to live an unlimited, happy, joyful experience.

Taking responsibility for your choices, because they're your choices is the only true justification for a choice. The reasons for your choice are not as important as the fact you made the choice and it's your responsibility to understand what choices you want and what choices will serve you best.

CHAPTER EIGHTEEN

LYING TO YOURSELF

ALTHOUGH I DON'T BELIEVE any mentally sane or competent person has the true ability to lie to him or herself, I do believe we have the ability to convince ourselves, through justifications of our behaviors, that the way we behave is acceptable. We've come to believe it's better to produce justification for our behaviors and thoughts than to admit we're not behaving and thinking in a manner we actually desire.

External support for our justifications of just about any type of behavior or thought is readily available from others. If you can't find it in one place, keep looking. You'll find it in another. This makes it easy to convince ourselves of the rightness of our behaviors and thoughts, even though they don't reflect who we want to be.

We can commit a crime. While we can't tell ourselves it wasn't a crime, we can convince ourselves it was justified. Most of the misconceptions and lies of life are born in our abundant imaginations, which we use to justify being a person we don't want to be. The stronger of us then propagate these lies to others, through our influences. We convince others to agree with the opinions we've created, to justify being an individual we don't want to be.

This produces a support structure, which can be used to justify behaviors or opinions that would otherwise make us look wrong or bad, to ourselves and to others. This is today's society at its worst. We're living lies that we have somehow been convinced are acceptable. To become the person you want to be, you must be strong and do that which makes you that person, instead of doing that which makes you look good to others.

The more you deny the truth, the more the conflict of truth is within you. This includes lying to ourselves. Conflict of truth is confusion. The more we want to be one thing, the more confused we are about decisions we make to be someone or something else.

We produce more lies, to camouflage how we really feel about ourselves. Soon, we're wondering if life has any worth. We begin to hide behind the lies of what we are, just to be accepted.

If you state your truth, you'll find people who are intrigued and enchanted by the truth and by your courage to display it. Truth rings real and truthful for all of us.

When you confess the truth about who you are and who you want to be, through your behaviors and how you experience life, you'll see different reactions and behaviors from people. Some people will want to understand. Others will fight to find a way to make your truth fit their teachings of what should be real. Still others will fear you and scorn you, not believing any possibility that life is or can be wonderful, when experienced from the understanding of your point of view. It all depends on other peoples' experiences in their own lives and their needs to hold onto their own fears. These are the motivations that produce behaviors to protect them from looking wrong, from feeling they have failed to understand something.

Leaders state their truths or influence others to believe in their lies. Intelligent, open minds find it refreshing to be in the company of someone who sincerely displays truths they've been convinced didn't exist, truths they've always desired. Weak minds, or minds that have been trained and taught nothing better, follow and accept lies, in order to fit in and not look bad, always seeking a reason for life, rather than the experience of life itself.

A leader isn't necessarily someone who runs some type of organization. A leader is someone who thinks for him or herself. Others are attracted to this individual because of the truth, which is part of their existence.

Lying to ourselves is the most damaging lie there is, as it negatively affects our self worth. When we lie to others, we're basically lying to ourselves and must then try to justify how the behavior of lying will produce some benefit for us. I've heard many people try to justify lying. They must have spent a lot of time and mental effort finding reasons and convincing themselves, before they had the confidence to state it out loud, as one of their principles of life. Only truth can produce the ability to never have to think about something beyond the fact it is true.

Catholics believe in confession. Confession occurs when individuals freely and openly admit to themselves that something in their lives was not, or is not, being handled in a manner that is truthful for who they desire to be as a person. Confession, outwardly or to ourselves, relieves our minds of the confusion that's produced when we try to justify behaviors that don't truthfully produce the person we want to be. To admit you're wrong relieves you of the efforts to convince yourself you could be right. Confess your mistakes and let them go. Pay more attention to the truth, than to justifying your lies. Only in truth is there peace and peace of mind.

CHAPTER NINETEEN

CONVERSATIONS

HAVE YOU EVER HEARD the phrase, "It's only a conversation." If you have, you know more than I did most of my life. The phrase means, most of the time, that words alone have no true consequence. We make a choice, in most conversations, to allow the words being spoken to have some affect, meaning or consequence. Our interpretation of the words and conversation are often influenced by our habits.

I might tell a friend he smells like garlic, probably because he recently ate something containing a great deal of the spice. His response might be to ask if his odor offends me. I've not said it offends me, I've only observed the fact he smells like garlic. While this may seem obscure, the point is that his interpretation of my comment is different from what I meant to convey.

Our experiences have made us very proficient at interpreting innuendos and subtleties in conversation, as well as sometimes not so subtle nonverbal communication. These nonverbal communications are real and expected parts of everyday life. How do we respond to commonly accepted communications, which require us to interpret their intended meaning, in order to accurately and truthfully function in society?

Once again, you respond with behaviors and thoughts that produce the person you desire to be.

Let's go back to the conversation about the garlic odor. My friend's response was a reasonable question and may represent his concern that he doesn't wish to offend or disturb anyone who finds the smell of garlic undesirable. However, depending on what experiences an individual has had and what stories are playing in his or her mind, the response could be interpreted as an accusation their odor is offensive and a rude, nasty comment. At that point, miscommunications begin to fly.

Making up stories in our heads, about the meaning behind someone else's words, is not seeking the truth. It's a lot of wasted effort. Respond to conversations with behaviors and interpretations that produce and reflect the person you desire to be. This doesn't necessarily provide the truth about what others mean, but it does produce a more functional way to have conversations. If you're happy and you realize it's not your responsibility if others are incapable of communicating their real intentions, you benefit from not wasting your energy on the false parts of other peoples' lives.

Experience has taught us how to respond to conversations. We don't look at the truth that conversations are interpreted to have to have importance. Granted, many conversations are important. However, many conversations we stress over have no true, physical, measurable consequence. If I tell someone he or she is an idiot, the truth is that nothing has really happened. Whether or not the statement has merit, it can only have consequence if someone chooses to give it consequence. If we choose to ignore a comment or statement, for whatever reason, nothing comes of it. We have control over how we choose to let life and conversations affect us.

I'm not saying words or conversations can't have physical affects or consequences, based in a reality or truth. Conversations that decimate character can have real consequences. Conversations can sometimes result in a loss for someone. However, most conversations are just words, which we can choose how to experience.

The more I live my life defined for myself, the less negative influence other peoples' conversations have over me. I refuse to let conversations, which have no real affect on my life, control or influence my experiences. Even someone who is very important in my life is not allowed to control my existence.

If my wife were to call me an idiot – and I'm sure if she hasn't already done so, she will at some point – it would hold very little weight for me, although I'd likely try to find out what's bothering her, to cause such a comment. However, because I base who I am on my principles, not hers, if I can confirm I am being the person I desire to be, her judgment of who I am and how I behave isn't going to influence my behaviors or happiness.

My influences are my principles. Living by and living up to my principles is my character. I get my self worth from knowing my character provides me the ability to make choices which can produce my desires. My self worth provides the confidence that I'm a happy person, who is experiencing a beautiful life. Even though my wife is very important to me, I don't give her the power to make choices over how I experience my life. Why, then, would I let people who are less important to me have any power over how I experience my existence?

In our society, we've been taught that what other people say to us and about us is important and has some meaning or affects on our existence. We tend to react unproductively to useless conversations, because we want to look as though we respect ourselves to a degree we think others will find appropriate. The truth is, most conversations have no affect on our lives, unless we allow them to do so, by reacting as if they had the influence to produce some consequence.

Unless I experience a true tangible, ethical or moral loss, I have the ability to not let other peoples' words make me react in a way that doesn't serve me, by behaving in ways that don't make me who I want to be. Allowing conversations to control my behaviors is refusing to accept responsibility for whom and what I am. The fact that I have the power, control, influence and ability to shape my own existence, through my own choices, based in my desires to be the type of person I want to be, is something I can use for my benefit.

You can test this for yourself. Listen to conversations, but don't react to them. Just listen. Most of the time, if you don't react to the conversation in a negative manner, it will have no true negative consequences for you. You have the control and make the choice. Often, we can use our choice of how to behave to influence a negative situation in a positive manner and provide an educational example for the people around us. When this occurs, people learn to constructively produce desired communication experiences.

CHAPTER TWENTY

WIN – WIN

"WIN-WIN" DESCRIBES A SITUATION in which all parties and participants involved come away from the situation satisfied with the resolutions. It is another phrase widely used and defined long ago by others than myself.

To understand this phrase, we need to understand the universe is, as far as we know, infinite. This infinite supply of materials and choices allows us to keep looking for solutions to situations and issues that produce win-win results

The infinite not only has relevance for space and matter but, more importantly, it exists in the mind as creativity. This is why there is my way of doing something, your way of doing something and an infinite number of additional possibilities or solutions. The Law of Free Will allows everyone to make choices, regarding how to attain their desired experience of life. The Law of the Infinite allows for no limits to our choices, although we tend to create such limits ourselves.

This means that to accept a situation other than win-win, such as lose-lose or win-lose or lose-win, is ignorant and lazy. Life is not a pie with limited resources. We don't need to measure how much we get, if we get enough or if others get some also. We need to recognize this and stop obsessing over whether we're getting enough or taking more than we need. We must stop thinking there's no way everyone can experience what they desire in their existence.

In Western societies, we're trained to be winners or we're losers. In this type of society, if one is to win, another must lose. I consider this de-facto, unconscious behavior a sad and poor excuse for humanity. Why should others not experience their winning life, in order for someone else to have one? Observe this behavior in the world and you'll see the horror of aggression, the belittlement of human self worth and outright, conceited, arrogant, selfish and nasty behavior, with no love or consideration for anyone. Observe a child's sporting event. It's very clear, in most cases that teaching what it means to win can create horrible human beings, because of how we're taught what it means to lose.

I don't think sports are a negative behavior, nor do I think doing better than someone else is negative. Competition creates efforts, which allow the human ability to achieve more. Comparison is what relative reality is all about. However, our society behaves in a manner that makes winning more important than mentoring. We allow unevenly trained or matched humans, especially children to compete, then gauge their ability or worth by such competition. This is an abomination of intelligence and certainly not what our true souls desire to experience.

If we could teach those with greater abilities to mentor and guide, rather than conquer and control, the world could be filled with greater abilities. I've observed that when you think you're greater or better than the person next to you, you've failed. Only when you decide that your strengths are your opportunity to mentor and teach will you have success and self worth that can never be taken away from you, whether or not you're winning at the game of the moment.

Creating situations and finding conclusions that produce desired results for everyone involved is the true WIN. Destroying someone else, in order to win and look better than them, so you can look good to your world, is worse than selfish, worse than cruel. It's weak. It's much harder and takes more strength to produce advantageous results for the masses than to do the simple and easy thing for yourself, forgetting we aren't alone in this experience.

CHAPTER TWENTY ONE

LIFE IS AN EXPERIENCE

HAVING THE COURAGE TO make the choices that produce the person you want to be isn't always easy. It often means going against society's norms. Peer pressure from friends, family and society often goes against the choices we need to make, in order to find fulfillment. Living life, by making choices based on our principles, can alienate those around us. They will usually desire, if not require, that we make choices based on what they've been taught to believe is best, regardless of whether or not they're truly enjoying their life.

Many of us have placed a great deal of importance on finding a meaning to life, hoping this meaning will guide us to make choices which will produce a happy and fulfilled life. When and if we detour from the choices a selected meaning defines for us, we experience one more aspect of negative feelings about ourselves, derived from our inner consciousness of not choosing what we've been taught to choose. We experience judgments and expectations of the foundation in which we put our faith and whose standards we're not meeting. We judge ourselves as weak and undeserving, because we fail to live up to some meaning of that which we've been taught.

While I would never deter someone from their religious pursuits and beliefs, I'd like to point out what I've learned from my studies of the meaning of life. Since I began studying, with point of view always in mind, the one conclusion that comes up consistently is that life is an experience. Although choices have consequences, any experience that doesn't harm you, go against your personal principles or cause harm or pain to another person or thing is part of life. The experiences of our lives need not be limited by other influences.

Life is an experience, so experience it!

Living life as an experience, and experiencing as much as you can, is the greatest glorification you can give the universe.

A key to living life as an experience is control. You must control your life, rather than letting life control you. This doesn't mean you can control the physical laws of the universe. It means you understand them and use them to your benefit.

I surf. I do not control the waves, but I can use them and ride them for my pleasure. The more I understand the dynamics of ocean waves, the more I can control my experience. The better I understand observed truths about this sport I love, the greater my control and ability to perform at it and enjoy it, creating possibilities for high levels of experiences.

If I believed in God, and I do in a certain context, I observe through my teachings that the greatest glorification of this God is to experience life. To create, through these experiences of my existence, something new, something which has never been created before. Whether it's a physical item or mental thought, creativity is the ultimate glorification of a creator. That which we create can be compared to the creation of existence itself, which allows for the creation of this universe to have a greater reference to its own beauty.

The wider the gap between glory and evil, good and bad, hot and cold, small and large, the greater the comparison for each relative condition becomes. If there were only the possibility of a difference in temperature of one degree, there would be too little difference for comparing temperatures. The greater the possible difference in temperature, the greater the comparison of difference can be.

Since we live in a relative world, where the infinite can exist, I can always add one to any number to make it larger. The possible comparison of glory to evil has no limits. The possibility of what can be created has no limits in a universe that contains the infinite.

The experience of creation is the ultimate experience of existence.

I've observed that all faiths and spiritual contexts with which I've become familiar reach the same conclusion. Life is an experience. I've also observed that such faiths and spiritual contexts explain that experiencing your life is what you're here to do. What better way to glorify a creator than to take full advantage of this experience he's provided us?

CHAPTER TWENTY TWO

EXISTENCE

WHAT IS EXISTENCE AND what does it mean? For me, it means I'm here, writing this book. I have this experience of my life, nothing more and nothing less. Existence must have always been. I see no way you can create something from literally nothing. It would seem a self-evident truth that existence must have been and will always be, in some form. Existence may not seem like a nuts-and-bolts things to discuss, but it is, if I wish to discuss subjects such as the supernatural and miracles. I must first be able to define these words.

When we try to conceive the idea that something can come from nothing, the logic doesn't hold up. If you can truly behold nothing, if that nothingness can truly exist, try to imagine how something can be created from this nothingness. Again, this isn't logically or even theoretically possible.

The fact I'm writing this book means I exist. The fact you're reading it means you exist. We may exist in some other way than we currently understand, but we still exist. If you can't create something from nothing, then existence, in some form and manner, has always been and will always be.

To ponder the beginning or end of existence is a futile act. We can understand the beginning and end of us, as we exist at the moment, but the idea that the existence of everything came from nothing is an impossible reality.

For those of you who believe in miracles or supernatural acts, I'd ask you to define what the two words mean. According to Webster, a miracle is "an event that seems to be scientifically unexplainable; a supernatural occurrence."

I challenge anyone to scientifically explain anything completely. For every answer you give to any question, another question is created. Somewhere, the explanations for our existence will all point back to the precise moment of the beginning of our universe and I will then ask, "What came before that?"

You could respond with the spiritual answer that God was before that and I would ask you to explain where God came from.

The point of all this is that either everything is a miracle or there are no miracles. It all depends on point of view. Again, nothing can be completely scientifically explained. This includes that nothingness can't ever exist. In other words, what created existence? And what created that which created existence? It's an infinite question. I'm not here to discuss faith. I wish to convey the understanding and ideas of process. Somewhere we must say it is as it is, without proof, and just have faith. Otherwise, we'll find ourselves forever searching for answers and will fail to experience this existence.

Okay, nothing is supernatural. Webster's definition of the word is "existing outside the forces of nature; miraculous." I challenge anyone to find something outside the forces of nature. Even if humans, or other intelligent, sentient beings, produce it, this is only us manipulating nature. Since I am man and part of nature, then all I am and all I produce are part of nature. Even global warming is just a natural part of human existence.

The point is, while we exist, we'll eventually have to just have faith that existence can never be fully explained. Dealing with the realities of our existence, the things we can influence and experience, is a far more likely way to obtain some purpose for living, than hoping there's magic in the universe that will some day explain its workings and plans for our existence.

Free will has left us with our own responsibilities for what we'll experience. No miracle or supernatural event is going to shine a light of understanding on us, explaining some greater reason for our existence. Even God, Himself, is subject to the laws of this universe He created when He is in it. Otherwise, He destroys His creation, as we're currently aware of it. Faith comes into play sooner or later, no matter how scientifically you like to see things.

Wasting time and energy on subjects beyond our ability to understand or influence is not the way to acquire desired experiences. We exist at the mercy or privilege of the universe and its laws.

The relative world is not one of two poles, but a world of three poles. Our universe is not two dimensional, but three dimensional. The left and right exist, but so do all the points in between. Positive and negative exist, but so does neutral. We have electrons, protons and neutrons.

Since there is the third possibility, since one more can always be added to the current number and since something can always be cut in half, the possibilities of our existence are infinite.

Our existence, through the Law of Free Will, allows us to always find new or different ways to do something. If one way doesn't work for us, there's most likely another way that will. This leaves us with the conclusion that existence can be what we desire it to be and only we limit the possibilities of our existence.

CHAPTER TWENTY THREE

EDUCATION AND KNOWLEDGE

L ET'S BE HONEST ABOUT knowledge. It's the only thing we really have. It's the only thing we have any possibility of taking with us beyond our current existence. Life is experience and knowledge is what we gain from this experience. Knowledge isn't always truthful. We can often learn and hold onto knowledge that doesn't help us or improve our lives.

Observe how much you truly know. Very few of us test the knowledge we're given. Most of what we know and understand is either the result of deductive thought or second hand information, provided by someone or something other than personal observation. We have little actual proof that what we think we know is true.

Be willing to say, "I don't know," so you'll have the opportunity to find the truth. Not only does this allow the possibility of an outside influence to educate you, it allows you to free up the energy and confusion that results from having to look like you know something, when you truly don't understand it.

In searching for the truth, don't let others convince you of a desire for something you know your soul is telling you is not what you want to experience. If information you acquire conflicts with a desire it's often because someone or something is simply restating that which they've been told. While there are sources of truthful information, don't hesitate to question information that conflicts with your desires. Require proof from your sources, so you can alleviate confusion in your life. Knowledge is only useful if it is truthful.

Knowledge is a personal achievement. It can't be given or provided by someone else. A book or other sources of information, explained or described to you by someone else, will provide information that's out of context or incomplete. To gain knowledge through understanding, you must read the book or gain the knowledge first-hand. Other people can provide insight to ideas you may not have considered, but they can't determine what you may have missed from a particular source.

Context is a very important aspect of knowledge. If something is taken out of context, it's easily perceived differently than originally intended. If I were to read you just one sentence or a few paragraphs or even just one chapter of this book, most of the understanding I'm communicating would be lost. You'd be left with only the ability to draw conclusions, regarding the book, based on misinformed knowledge of its contents.

The same is true for faiths and religions. If you don't read the entire work for yourself, the context in which something is explained must be taken on faith alone that the person or source explaining it is being truthful. I've never observed someone with the ability to explain a work of faith or religion, without adding his or her own interpretation of the ideas and presenting ideas out of context.

What has allowed me to come to my current understanding and point of view is my desire to experience knowledge first hand, as much as possible. I have no need for someone else to tell me what's real. I can determine this for myself, by educating myself with the truths of my existence.

CHAPTER TWENTY FOUR

ARGUMENTS

WHY ARE THERE SO many arguments in life? Is it because we all seem to have different opinions on things? I think not. Sure, we have different points of view. We often have a hard time understanding that someone can see something differently that we do and still be correct or that his or her idea may have merit. I think we argue, especially in close relationships, because we don't know how to communicate to each other what we want and desire.

Few of us can explain to ourselves what we want, much less articulate it to someone else. We live with habits that don't work truthfully. We live in confusion that creates doubt. We feel we must protect our image by proving, futilely, that we know what we're talking about, when we don't.

Face it, we're wrong and know so little, but we want others to believe we know. We grab onto the clichés of life, which have been regurgitated to us over the years, and we try to make them work. We never think about how little proof we have that any of these snappy and prestigious sounding clichés have any merit of truth in them. We have standards and expectations for our lives, which are necessary, despite the fact they can get in the way of our happiness. We lack the understanding that communicating our desires and expectations to our close relations is important and we don't have the training to do so.

Most important, we need to know what our expectations are. We need to know who and what we want to be, in order to determine what expectations are necessary for our happiness. Then, we need to share them with the important people in our lives, the people we want to trust and depend on. But trust and depend on to do what?

Think about any heated argument you've had with someone close to you and you may discover the issue was the argument. More than likely, the argument was about the other person not understanding who you are. And it's equally likely you've never communicated who you are, because you have no idea yourself.

You may think you've done a good job of communication your expectations, but most of us talk about what the world has taught us to discuss. We communicate expectations that make us look good, instead of the ones that make us understood.

Let's look at the issue of where you're going to live, as an example. You're in a marriage or a committed relationship and this is an important issue. If it was never discussed before the commitment was made, it can become the basis for destructive arguments, which usually lead to a feeling of not being understood. This feeling then becomes the issue in the argument, rather than the question of where to live, which is a major decision by itself.

However, rather than resolving this issue, you end up arguing about understanding each other. This leads to the feelings you can never resolve any issues in your relationship. Observe peoples' problems in relationship and you'll find two issues come up quite often. The first is the complaint of not being understood by the other. The second is that moving forward and resolving the issues never seem to happen.

"You just don't understand me," is overused and worthless. It has no meaning. If someone doesn't understand you, it's likely not his or her issue. It's yours, for not being able to communicate what's important to you. If, on the other hand, you do know what's important to you and have communicated that clearly, yet the other person doesn't honor that importance in a respectful way, maybe your issue is your choice of companion. Maybe it's time to let this person know how unacceptable his or her behavior is or maybe it's time to find someone who will honor you.

When we have a difference of opinion or a different point of view, we often get stuck in arguments that include the following statements. "You don't understand me. You don't know how important this is to me. After all this time, you don't get me. If you don't know, then I'm not going to tell you."

This is the biggest lie we've ever been taught. NO, we don't understand each other, unless and until we can explain ourselves to each other. We don't read minds. Most of us have no idea what expectations are best for us, so we regurgitate to others what we've been taught to believe is best.

I call this arguing about the argument. The issues we need to discuss are lost in the emotion of feeling we're not understood and this becomes the topic of the discussion. The more invested we are in the situation, the more intense the emotion and argument become. The longer we go, not informing important people in our lives of our true desires and expectations, the worse the situation becomes.

We're back to the main issue of confusion causing us negative issues in our lives. The confusion that results, when someone else communicates expectations that aren't truly what their soul is looking for, is the breeding ground for misunderstandings. Misunderstanding is the breeding ground for arguments.

There are enough real issues in life that must be discussed and compromised on. When they get hidden behind the emotion of not feeling understood, they never have a chance of being resolved. We spend all our energy screaming out our pain of not being loved enough to be magically understood.

There is no magic or, as I observe it, all the natural things of life are magic. Living within the laws of the spirit, as they are, is what will fix our soul's need to be understood. Find out who you are and find the courage to communicate the expectations you have, which are necessary to be whom and what you want to be.

In arguments, we often fall back into habitual behavior, learned at a very young age, which rarely produces the results we desire, as mature adults in mature relationships. When we find ourselves in arguments and negative situations, which produce undesirable feelings, we can construct a useful tool to not only eliminate confusion, but also help us use our ability to productively communicate.

The tool is your list of who you want to be. Instead of becoming defensive and accusatory, simple check your list of who you want to be and see if you've been everything you desire to be in the given role at the time of the issue. Most of the time, you'll find you're not making choices at this given time based on who and what you desire to be. Most of the time, if you behave, as you desire to, you'll be able to participate in difficult discussions and situations, without the confusion and doubts that often produce defensive behaviors which will not serve you.

If you've not been the person you desire to be and have checked your list, either during or after the situation, you'll find it easy to return and continue the situation in a manner that allows you to resolve the main issue. It's easy to recognize and correct ourselves and much easier to explain you're not being who you desire than it is to find reasons through your confusion to apologize.

Often we apologize to placate a person or ease a situation with no true understanding of why we're apologizing. Apologizing isn't bad, even when we don't understand why we're doing it, if it extinguishes a roaring fire and resolves a negative situation. It can be useful. However, it's much better to understand why we can make something better than it is to just bury and hide it inside of us, where it's left as fuel for use later, in another situation, or where it creates resentments of our lives.

There have been many times I've been sour-faced and angry with my wife, stuck in the argument and no longer dealing with the main issue, which was the basis for the situation. I've found that if I stop my habitual behavior, then take a moment to think of who I desire to be, I begin laughing at the funny looks of stupid anger on both of our faces, often guiding us back to dealing with the original issue, not dealing with the argument. Sometimes, we do this dance several times, going from anger to laughter to anger to laughter. It can be cute at times. The point is, we live in the moment, being who we desire to be, and stress the importance of not letting the other person's behaviors be the center of how we make choices for our own.

Key Lesson:

You'll find the elimination of confusion, surrounding knowing who you want to be, will eliminate many arguments and negative situations, if you react to situations based on your principles of being who you desire to be and not on the behavior of the other person.

Communicating with the important people in your life and coming to an understanding and/or compromise for your expectations in life will bring even more relief from confusion. Less of your energy will be spent arguing about arguments and you can put more effort and focus into solving the real issues of your existence.

Solving issues and moving on to other possibilities in your life is what gives you the opportunity and possibility to experience your desires.

When we behave lovingly, because that's who we desire to be, not just because someone is acting in a manner that encourages us to be loving, we have the possibility of creating an environment that is loving, even when someone else is not. Your other choice is to be nasty, when faced with nastiness, which you justify because it makes you look strong and good to others, even though it only serves to fuel the fire of a nasty environment.

I choose to be whom I desire to be based on my principles, not someone else's behaviors. The Law of Choice provides you with the power of influence, should you choose to use it. Stop thinking fighting fire with fire is a productive behavior or that it will help you achieve your desires.

I observe this simple understanding will produce more desired life experiences than any other understanding.

CHAPTER TWENTY FIVE

MIND/INTELLECT AND SOUL

THE IDEA OR CONCEPT I'm about to suggest may be hard to observe as truth, but I have, in fact, observed it to be true and have also observed the idea is a key for happiness.

One thing we're taught, in today's modern societies, is that using our intellect is the way to produce security and happiness. I've never observed this as being true. My observations have shown me using our intellect to calculate the choices we should make to be happy is one of the biggest fallacies we've come to depend on. Using our intellect to determine what will make us happy is like asking a hammer to build a house. The intellect is a tool.

The mind, the intellectual part of our being, isn't the same as the soul. The mind is a tool for use by the soul. Just as a computer doesn't provide purpose for its calculations, the mind doesn't provide purpose for its functions.

There are those who argue that all behaviors of existence are meant to provide for continued existence. We find ways to survive, so we can procreate and continue the species. I find it impossible to observe this as truth. I do observe, in many instances, human lives have more motivation factors than survival. I find this to be another self-evident truth.

Most of our lives, we're taught to use our intellect, or mind, to achieve our goals. That makes sense. However, we're also taught to use our minds to determine what we desire. I've never gotten a response from a hammer on how to build a house. To know what we desire, we must listen to our soul, our heart, and then use our tools, such as intellect, to achieve the desires of our soul.

The mind is like a sponge, with the ability to soak up and retain the experiences of our lifetime. For the majority of us, it has been the subject of primary attention for those who participate in providing guidance for our intellectual education.

The mind stores and calculates information, but its purpose is the survival of the body in which it resides. Without an idea of how to use this intellect, the mind is often confused. There are several reasons for this. One reason the mind lives in confusion is the lack of mentoring on the subject of truth, how to observe truth and how to live confidently with the truth.

Without a goal for the intellect to achieve, the mind becomes a useless tool, without a job. This leaves an educated intellect to search for reasons to exist and function, to search for and find almost any possibility, beneficial or detrimental, for the individual to exist.

If we exist only to assure the continuation of our species, why does the ability to question aspects of our existence exist? Nature doesn't produce useless behaviors. Any scientist or naturalist will tell you that. We are nothing more than part of the nature of our universe. Nature has elaborated, adjusted and modified behaviors to points of curious pondering of a behavior's evolution and characteristics, yet still retaining a relationship for the purpose for the behavior.

This leads to the conclusion that our abilities for esoteric, philosophical and seemingly impossible ideas must have some use and purpose. I've observed that such intellectual abilities have use, when it comes to manifesting the deepest desires of the human soul, to think beyond instinct and to provide satisfaction for the human desire to understand and create.

Why is there a need to understand and create? I'm not going to waste your time or mine proving we have this desire. It is an obvious observation and any one of us can observe the fact.

How much of a purpose or need is there to just continue existing with the same old things? If nothing changes, why struggle to be at all? Everything we'd need to know would eventually be figured out, leaving no reason for individuality. However, what if I can do something completely new? If there are no limits to the possibilities of my ideas, the universe can continue with everyone being able to discover and create and no basis or law for ending existence is then possible.

The gauge with which possibility is measured will forever exist and grow. The idea of what is wonderful will always have the potential of becoming more wonderful. Thus, a way has been provided which allows the greatness of the wondrous existence of a creator, God or universe to become infinitely greater.

If I were to create a way to be praised, I'd do it in a way that would allow no limits for such praise.

Believe it or not, you've always known this about your existence. It's an old understanding and one that has gotten such little attention from anything you experience you either gave up on the usefulness of the knowledge or stopped paying it any attention.

Whatever the truth is that drives us to have desires above and beyond survival or to create unique manifestations of our being's esoteric ideas, these desires are from the soul. This is the soul's way of communicating to the body and mind the need to put forth efforts to experience its existence in this reality as a unique being. The desire of the soul is what we truly seek to achieve. When we ignore such desires, we create an existence, which isn't fulfilling.

Letting the mind control the existence of the soul is, as I've said, like asking a hammer how to build something. The mind has no purpose, if there is no desire. The mind cannot desire, it can only deduce and reason. The body and soul have desires and depend on the intellect to help them achieve these desires.

There is no reasoning, when it comes to desires, for what our beings most crave to experience. I observe this is truly more a need than just desire and is beyond any tangible part of us or this universe to understand. If existence cannot be truthfully explained or understood, than neither can the desire for existence be a subject of explainable understanding.

We're often taught we can reason our way to happiness, but happiness is what it is. The greatest intellectual ability cannot replace our innermost desires. Denying that which we seek to experience only produces regret. Asking others to deny that which they desire only produces resentment. Desire comes from that unknown place within us, which I'm willing to call the soul.

If we teach our minds to be at the service of our souls and if we consciously accept our minds are tools, we can begin to understand the basic laws that exist. These allow for the human experience to be guided to an infinite possibility of an accomplished existence, which includes everything we know we desire to be.

Chapter Twenty Six

THE SOUL AND THE VESSEL

I want to discuss an idea of what our soul is, so we can speak in a common language with the entire world. For the purpose of our conversation, we can simply define a soul as the desires that exist within us. It is the soul we deal with, when we know we should behave or be a given way. It is the soul, which makes it impossible to justify to ourselves the idea that behaving in other ways can provide truthful fulfillment of our most desired experiences. It's not important for this definition of the soul to be agreed upon or accepted, so long as you know this is the definition I'm applying in this discussion and I don't include the mind or intellect in reference to the soul.

More for fun than need, I wish to discuss more deeply my ideas about the possible understandings of the soul. This chapter will deal with ideas of possibilities, not observations, as is the case with other chapters in the book.

This discussion is in no way meant to define a truth. It's a discussion of ideas, through examples of possibility. Where or how did I imagine some thoughts? In some cases, I asked a question and got an answer. In some case, it may even have been provided by some divine interventions. I avoid discussion of specific religious issues. My knowledge of such is mostly limited to my own efforts of self-education, restricting my qualifications on the subject. I've observed such discussions need the correct forum and often produce situations that focus on the religious issues of life, rather than any other subjects being discussed. I will, at times, use analogies and examples based in spiritual faiths to help convey an idea.

Let's begin with the idea of God and Soul. I see these two ideas as being one and the same, both from spiritual education and my own feeling. Everything that exists, and the only true thing is knowledge, is God, and our souls are a small piece of God. If you use an ocean as the image of God and as all there is to be consciously aware of for existence, you can then think of a glass filled with water from this ocean as a unique, individual soul. The water in the glass is the soul and the glass itself is the vessel or body.

The soul, the water in the container, can be pure or it can be contaminated in many different ways. In this case, we should understand that contaminated doesn't necessarily mean negatively contaminated and that I know of no pure souls.

I believe, truly believe, our self-awareness, or consciousness, is something of a continuing existence. I'm not going to hint that I could know any truth to such a statement, beyond observation. My observation is that existence is eternal, because nothing cannot exist and we cannot come from nothing and do not end as nothing, merely continue in some form or other.

Following this thinking, I would suggest that consciousness is like the ocean. When we're brought into this universe, a vessel scoops some water from the ocean of consciousness, pure at that moment, as far as the benchmark of what is already in the ocean. This vessel allows for a unique individual consciousness to begin. All the aspects of the greater body of consciousness are still part of the new individual consciousness, in at least some small way. However, at the moment of conception, a new, completely unique, consciousness begins its own path (I like to think of it as its own bath) and has the free will to experience and create, within the laws of the vessel's universe, as it chooses.

We'll discuss the glass, as an analogy for the vessels in which our souls must be contained, in order to experience this universe, in the next section. This section concentrates on the soul.

At conception, our vessel is metaphorically filled with a portion of the eternal consciousness. It becomes a unique individual, because the path from this point on is now separate and unique from the eternal consciousness and any other human consciousness. It now contains all the aspects, in some smaller proportions, of the larger ocean of consciousness. Remember, the ocean is God, the oneness, greater universal soul and eternal consciousness. The smaller portion becomes a unique individual's soul and is, in some small part, exactly the same as the greater universal soul of God and contains, in smaller proportions, all the aspects of the greater soul.

This idea allows for the conceptual understanding of how we can be a part of the universe's, or God's, larger understanding and possess their same abilities to understand and create. Many faiths believe we all are one with God in all desires and aspects and, through a deep faith or understanding, we have the abilities to preside over the existence we experience. The path of this unique being has free will to choose the experiences of its existence.

The soul can make choices that preserve its purity with certain experiences, ones no different than what it already understands, or it can contaminate or alter its purity with new experiences, creative and unique experiences, whether they're beneficial or detrimental for the health of the soul. The environment also influences the soul from conception, guiding it and diluting it with both truths and false understandings.

I have observed it's almost impossible to not contaminate our souls. This contamination isn't always or necessarily a negative contamination. We're here to experience unknown parts of existence. The new information and knowledge we gain changes us to something different and newer than the soul at conception. Some of what we experience will provide nourishment for our souls and existence. Other experiences will poison and dirty our understandings of existence. Thus, we become unique individuals, with common and different contaminants in our souls.

Once the soul is produced, as an individual in its vessel, it begins an existence that becomes unique, as it's guided by its choices and environment. Free will and the laws of the relative universe, in which it now exists, are the basic elements for the possible experiences it can manifest.

These experiences provide knowledge from a unique prospective. This knowledge builds new understandings, which can only be discovered separately from the original greater soul in a relative existence. The ability to be creative and produce a unique idea, which can be tested for its value and worth, through manifestations of creative ideas, allows for larger growth to the greater soul, or God, of what existence is and is possible of being.

The growth of the number of these types of beings with unique souls, whether unique to our world as humans or more proliferated, as in the possibility of sentient life in other places in our universe, multiplies the possibilities for this idea of new understandings of existence even more.

Souls go through their existence in this universe polluting their original composition, in terms of knowledge and understandings. When I say, "polluting," I mean changing their original composition. Many of the truths a soul may think it's discovering for the first time are actually memories of something it already knows, but some knowledge and understanding it creates or discovers is new and unique for both this soul and the greater understanding of our universe, the one greater soul and God.

Am I suggesting God can and does have something to learn beyond current understanding and knowledge? That's exactly what I'm saying. Just because you may know all there is to know at any given moment of existence, this doesn't mean it's not possible to create something new, which extends and/or increases what is currently a possibility. If I knew all there was to know, I have no problem believing I might desire to learn something new. The greater number of places with the possibility to produce more knowledge would only increase the ability and opportunities to satisfy this desire. Allowing for unique perspective and possibilities, beyond my own being, would allow for a much more interesting existence. I think our ability to create, with the same conceptual abilities as our creator, is only a logical deduction, with the understandings of spiritual faith that have been presented to this world.

Sometimes, similar, even exactly the same, experiences of new creativity may happen to different souls, without their knowledge. This still means that to these souls, the experiences are new and unique and creative. They may learn differently when they transition from this existence, which we define as death.

Souls go through their existence, hopefully producing productive new creations, but even new negative creations exist and have their place in our journey of knowledge. Through these creations and experiences, the smaller, unique body of the ocean is polluted with new knowledge and ideas. Upon transition, through death, back to the greater body of the ocean of the universal soul, they bring their unique perspectives or points of view and their creations to the one universal soul. This expands the current measure of what there is to know. This gives even an omnipotent being the ability to have reason to exist, through finding new possibilities for experiences it hasn't previously known.

This makes the idea of soul mates much more understandable, if we think of souls in this way. A soul mate is not one person's soul being uniquely compatible with just one other soul in this world of over six billion people. Soul mates are those who see similar or desirable qualities, experiences and knowledge in another soul.

You can think of it in terms of how the soul is polluted. As it is filled with more experiences, the water is colored to a certain extent. We have desires or preferences for certain colors and sometimes we find the colors similar to what we know to be comforting and desirable. The opposite may also be a true. A soul that is dark and cloudy, poisonous to life and rancid, is a soul of an existence filled with false, negative, uncreative and unrealized experiences, which has left the soul ugly and despairing. A clearer, more brilliantly colored soul is colored with pollutants that nourish life, positive, desired experiences with positive creativity abundant in its existence.

Not only are we attracted to like colors and experiences but, just as in our tangible and physical world, we are easily repelled by nasty, poisonous, rancid substances. A soul that is dark and cloudy is the soul of an existence filled with false, negative, uncreative and unfulfilled experiences, which has left it ugly and in despair.

We are, instead, attracted to refreshingly fragrant, beautifully colored, nourishing substances. A clear, more brilliantly colored soul, contains pollutants that nourish life, creating a soul, which has achieved a purer life, including positive desired experiences and positive creativity in its existence.

There are always exceptions, where some people enjoy the grossest parts of life and hate the sweetest, but this is what makes the world go around.

In soul mates, we find things in other peoples' souls that reflect our desires for our existence, black or white. We can also see how certain souls may be much more desirable or attractive to other souls, because of their purity. Some aspects of souls may be inherently observable, while others may take time and effort to become aware of. In addition, a soul's characteristics change over time, with the ever-continuing new experiences of the soul's existence. A soul we find desirable at one moment may change and not be what we desire at another time. A soul, which cannot grow at all, leaves us with a mundane soul with which to experience life. This could work for us, or not. Based on all this, you can see how the attraction of souls can be measured and understood.

We've seen an idea of how a soul for our universe is born into existence. Now, let's look at the idea of passing away, out of this relative existence, back to an existence of the universal soul or God.

When this happens, the soul is released from the rules, laws and confinements of this universe. The vessel a soul is traveling in, to survive in this relative universe, dies and the soul is released back to a different existence. The unique soul becomes instantly aware of all the universal knowledge of the one greater soul it came from and was once a part of, because the laws for that existence are different than the laws for existence in this universe. The aspects for knowledge could be extremely different.

Now, I don't want cups of dirty, nasty water being poured into my clean pond of water, with beautiful life in it. The analogy of a wasted life of experiences and negative, useless creations being added to the ocean of knowledge and life is the issue here. This being the case, a judgment is necessary. Compare this idea where you'd like it to fit into your spirituality.

We must start with the consideration that a new, unique being is in existence and separate from the universal soul it was first part of. While this new soul has returned to the original and universal soul, it is still separate and unique. It now remembers all of the understanding, everything there was to know about all existences, when it was born. It still has understanding of free will, whether or not this law exists in the universal soul's plane of existence. The new soul may have a desire to continue on as a unique soul, in some manner of existence. If this is so, there may be a way for this soul to not die, dying so by being returned to the greater universal soul and losing its unique and separate existence.

We understand death in our universe. Spirituality often refers to ever-lasting life in the hereafter or the death of the soul, from judgment of unworthiness to receive ever-lasting life.

Think of dying in the after life as throwing the water of a unique being's vessel into the ocean. The second the water hits the ocean, you can never retrieve the same exact glass of water. Even if you collect a fresh glass of water as quickly as you can, you'll retrieve a different, unique, glass of water. It may be similar in many ways. It may contain, in small parts, the original aspects of the universal, as well as any newly added aspects, which were added when knowledge from the unique soul was emptied back into the ocean. Still, the newly filled vessel will contain water which will be different and the unique soul, which was emptied back into the universal soul, will be lost forever to all possibility of ever existing again.

Once we return to God, as one with him again, we cease to exist. We die for all eternity, an everlasting death. This is not necessarily a negative prospect. It could be desired, but it could also be a judgment. It could be desired because the universal soul is familiar to it and the unique soul may have missed being a part of this and desire to be joined with it again. Maybe this is why we want to connect to other souls, here in this universe. Maybe we miss the connection of oneness, for whatever reason. Maybe it's familiar and comforting to us.

Before I continue, I want to explain this is a good analogy for understanding why the human experience desires to return, in any way it can, to a connection with other souls. It once was one, known as the singularity, of the greater consciousness and it has been proven, time and time again, that like migrates to like.

Let's go back to the idea that I don't want dirty water thrown back into my pool, which I'm responsible for keeping alive. Here is where the idea of judgment of our existences comes into understanding.

Imagine that all souls will have all the knowledge, ability and understanding of the idea of a universal soul or God. All of this exists at the time judgment is needed, as to whether or not this unique glass of water will be allowed to rejoin the ocean of the universal soul. The decision will be based on the usefulness of any of its newly created aspects of knowledge and understandings, which occurred in our universe.

This unique soul will possess the same ability to justly judge as any other soul, including the universal soul. Self-judgment is then possible, making any judgment necessary for maintaining the purity of a universal non-coercive.

A righteous judgment of ourselves is the only way to truly reach a completely informed verdict. There could be many choices for a soul to select from, for its continuing existence, such as continuing existence in the sense of a unique soul or returning to the oneness existence from which it came.

A soul could return to the greater oneness as it is and share and add its experience to the universal soul, extending the understandings of all existence. It might prefer to continue as a unique soul, perhaps sharing a splash of its experience with the greater soul and grabbing back a small amount of the greater soul to replace this splash, gaining knowledge it may have missed while experiencing a different existence, before moving on to some other life, universe or unique experience.

With these possible choices, it would have to judge itself worthy to do so, based on the remaining amounts of purity, positive and useful knowledge of experiences and the understanding it can make choices beneficial to this unique soul, thus continuing on to greater experiences of positive creation. Even if the soul isn't perfect, the choice is there, so long as it's not so negatively polluted as to cause adverse contamination for the greater, universal soul. These judgments would most likely come to souls who have lived an existence of beneficial achievement, showing they can continue on this path of existence.

A soul might judge itself not worthy to continue on, because of the negative contaminates it's collected from an existence of negative experiences. It may decide the pollutants, at least in full strength, have no benefits for a truthful understanding of existence. This judgment outweighs any new, useful understandings or knowledge it may have to share with the greater existence. It may decide it doesn't have an ability to produce positive experiences for the soul and should be removed from its unique existence and mixed back into the ocean of oneness, available for other possibilities of existence.

There is a sad catch with this choice. Although only a very small part, a tiny splash, of this negatively polluted soul may be shared with the greater soul, to assure what has been uniquely experienced is never lost, this soul cannot continue on or be returned to the greater soul as it is. Still, it must somehow return to the greater soul. It has nowhere else to exist and reached this verdict for itself. This judgment includes the fact it is not to pollute the greater soul, where it must return.

Obviously, a cleansing of the waters of the unique soul is necessary. How would we clean this pollution? Would we use chemicals? I think not, as these are just more pollutants and most cleansing chemicals have adverse affects and are destructive to life. Purification, as much as possible, would be most advantageous, without adding or leaving behind chemicals.

The best way I know to purify water, or just about anything else, is with heat and fire. Burn the soul until it's cleansed, then return the purified water back to the greater, universal soul. Or than one might let this unique soul, which has not lost all understanding of its unique experiences, return to some unique existence. It may sound awful, but it's an understanding for many horrifying spiritual ideas, which have been put forth in our existence. When understood this way, it may be a much more logical way to perceive why something may need to be explained in such a manner that it appears scary and awful.

Hopefully, our beings retain their experiences in some way. Otherwise, life is a waste of time.

This idea of the soul is meant only to provide an example of an explanation of possibility. We're looking for possibility from points of looking for truth. I'm not trying to suggest this is how the existence of anything, much less the soul, exists, either truthfully or conceptually or that the idea relates to any faith or belief. The more I open my mind to possibility, the easier it becomes for me to recognize how beautiful certain aspects of existence really are.

The vessel represents the body or physical elements of our existence. The soul, or spirit, is the self-aware creative essence, which produces purpose for sustaining the vessel. The vessel is what allows a consciousness to exist in this universe and experience relative possibilities. The body is only a ship, although it's an amazing ship, with complex machinery and dynamic processors.

I believe – and this is only my belief – that existence doesn't require a vessel but, within our known universe, the only way we can exist, to travel and manifest creativity with relativity, is through a physical existence.

In the preceding section, we used a glass or cup to represent the vessel or body. The glass itself is the vessel and the content within the vessel is the soul. Again, we used water, because of its unique properties, to represent the contents of the vessel, the soul.

There are many types of containers that can be a vessel. Cups and glasses made of glass, plastic, ceramic or wood. These may be large or small, clear or colored, smooth or bumpy, symmetric or unique, whole, cracked or broken. You can see how this vessel could represent different types of physical humans, different types of beings' bodies.

The vessel grows from its genetic design and environmental influences. The differences between vessels are obvious and can be observed in the diverse cultural and ethnic characteristics of human bodies.

Both the body and the soul grow from design and environment, becoming a unique existence for each person. The more we understand the laws and processes governing how each part of the body and soul exist, the healthier we make each one. Studies, leading to understanding what the body requires for health, have been and continue to be done almost constantly. It's easy to find resources to help produce a healthier physical existence for our bodies. However, we must remember that while the soul requires the body for existence in this universe, the soul is only a passenger, whether a captain or tourist. The body doesn't define purpose. It only allows for manifestations to be created and experienced.

CHAPTER TWENTY SEVEN

PLEASURE

PLEASURE IS SUCH A... well... pleasurable word. It conjures up images of warm, sunny days, massages, ice cream, beaches and orgasms. Pleasure is the point between sensation and pain. Physical, intellectual, spiritual and emotional pleasures all exist within the same tolerances.

When you're getting a massage, or just a back rub, if someone rubs lightly or tickles you, it may be a good, even pleasurable, sensation. However, especially when we're fatigued, we often desire a little more pressure. If that pressure is too hard, particularly in that sore spot, where we need it rubbed most, it can send us through the roof with pain.

During sex, not enough pressure where you need it may just feel nice. Too much pressure and, once again, you go through the roof with pain. However, rub that spot just the right way and... I leave that image up to your imagination.

Intellectually, it's nice to have problems to solve. We can even say the joy we feel when we've resolved a difficult problem is pleasure. However, if the problem is way beyond our abilities to resolve, it then becomes torturous or painful to deal with it. If a problem is far too easy to resolve, we often end up bored.

When we love someone, it's pleasurable to be in love just enough to desire the relationship, but not so much that you can't live your life without the relationship. That would be too painful. However, if the level of love is such that you could care less whether or not you're with the other person, this isn't fulfilling either.

We all have different thresholds for pain and sensation for all aspects of our being. Many of us close ourselves off to finding and understanding these thresholds. We need to know what they are, in order to understand how to find the comfortable places in our pleasure zones. Many don't know that pleasure is just before the point of pain and have no idea that this is how to find it. Yes, I have tested this, mostly with woman, and have observed it is true.

Many of our past experiences prevent us from allowing good and capable people in our lives their humanity and mistakes, which are inconsequential. These are necessary for discovering our thresholds for the possibilities of our desired experiences. When we're not living in the moment and not realizing a few mistakes can be used to guide us to greater and more pleasurable existences, we're hiding behind the walls of our fears. This keeps us from our desires. To trust someone or something, you must look beyond mistakes and flaws, small and earnest mistakes and flaws, to experience the goodness of pleasure.

Different points of view for the discovery of our pleasure points produce an existence than can not only meet our expectations, but also exceed them. The trust and surrender we give to the important people in our lives, to care for us, even though they may stumble on occasion, is rewarded by experiences we would never have thought of or wouldn't have thought possible.

CHAPTER TWENTY EIGHT

SEX AND PLEASURE

MEETING, LOVING AND MARRYING my wife was the beginning of my observations of the truth about sex and love. Until my third marriage, the information I was provided, both through other points of view and personal experiences, conflicted with what my soul told me should be real. I was provided false information regarding the realities of the true possibilities of the pleasure of sexual experiences. What a waste of time and pleasure! However, I've observed a more realistic truth. Even sex has no limitations.

What I believed to be true about sex was confirmed when I read a book by Rabbi Shmuley Beteach, titled *Kosher Sex*. I believe we all have something to learn from this man's point of view regarding sex. Did you think the big Kabala trend in celebrity circles is about spiritual awareness? It's possible, but really good sex is an amazing experience and I'm sure this is the primary motivation behind the trend. Tutors who provide truthful knowledge for a rewarding understanding of sex are rare, are often misunderstood and criticized for their teachings and point of view.

The Jewish faith sees sex as the highest form of earthly spirituality and, as I've observed, I share this view. It's as close as you can get to another person. The Jewish faith explains it's as close as you can get to touching God, while in this life.

This understanding goes along with the idea of our soul's desire to experience a union of souls it was once familiar with in some other understanding. The soul, which resides inside each of us, cannot touch another soul. Souls can communicate with each other, through emotional and mental intimacy, but the only way they have any possibility of touching is through sex.

If the soul is truly an inner subject to our vessels, reaching inside each other is the only way close to them touching, while on this physical plane.

Sex can bring opposites together, disrupt entire countries, and cause great men to do corrupt things, allow us to forget everything or finally feel at peace with the universe.

I hope the information I offer will provide a deeper and more meaningful way to express love through sex for those women who don't deeply enjoy it and for those men who misuse sex for selfish conquests. I hope the information will finally produce for these individuals the amazing experience we all feel should have always been possible.

There are over six billion people in the world and I'm sure there are as many differing needs, when it comes to what is good or right for them where sex is involved. There are many good texts on the mechanics of sex and just as many that are lousy, just as there are common and differing points of views. I'm not going into the issues of all the different ways and needs. I'm sure that's been covered extensively. What I will discuss is the underlying need and desire, as well as the common way to learn what is desired and good for any situation.

First and foremost, sex is a spiritual thing in today's societies. Take the spirit out of the equation and sex has negative consequences. Like happiness, sex begins with physical issues. In this case, it's the process of procreation and the pleasure of sensations of relief and satisfaction. However, for it to become a truly wonderful experience, sex must be looked at from a spiritual point of view.

Obviously, sex has accomplished its purpose of procreation. Billions of humans are sufficient proof of that. We've gone beyond that. Today sex is about an experience that goes beyond having babies. If all we want out of sex is an experience of our physical sensations, we could easily satisfy our desires through self-gratification, masturbation. However, the majority of us continue to desire the connection of another human. We want to be judged as having some worth to another person or soul.

For this reason, sex must have a much deeper purpose than just physical gratification. One could argue sex is about power, conquest and looking good to others. I've observed these motivators are backed by a lot of data to support them as true. More careful observation shows that such motivators are not the most fulfilling reasons to engage in sexual intimacy.

A simple test can prove that making love is a better motivator for sex than any other. Ask any male human which of the following is more satisfying. Making love to a woman who desires him to sexually pleasure her, who surrenders to him, who reacts to his sexual contact with great pleasure and climaxes and who gets emotionally lost in the moment of being together, or making love to a woman who just lays back and gets it over with, so the man can get off.

Ask any woman if she desires to be attracted to a man, in many different ways, in order to desire sexual intimacy from him. A woman desires a man's ability and efforts to take care of her, be kind to her, consider her desires and needs and find her unique and desirable.

This should be enough to prove that making love is a deeper motivator than just having sex. Using sex to consummate love, turning sex into lovemaking, is the closest two humans can come to touching each other's souls.

If we can agree that making love is the greatest reason for sexual intimacy, we can take a look at what making love is really about.

Making love is about the connection, acceptance and closeness people desire from others. It's about getting to know someone, without guards being put up to hide the truth of who they are and who they desire to be. It is being so close, so accepting, that the bodily areas and fluids, which generally offend us, become desirable. Lovemaking is a time when, no matter how goofy we may be acting, we're allowed to show this side of us. If our trust and confidence is betrayed, it can be the place that brings great grief into our lives.

Intimate sexual experiences are different from just having sex. Being intimate, opening up to and giving one's self to another during sex, is much more than just allowing sex to happen. I've observed no one who cannot tell the difference between the two experiences.

Intimate sex is fulfilling. Sex alone gets old and boring and there's no satisfaction in it, after time goes by. Lovemaking is opening up to another, allowing our interests to be shared and experienced and, hopefully, desired. In this way, we build on the experiences of lovemaking, instead of enduring the same old experience of sex that easily gets mundane and old.

For many of us, sex is disappointing from the start, never producing an experience we expected, hoped for and dreamed of. Seldom does it produce any possibility of satisfying our desires over the course of our sexual experiences. These types of sexual experiences leave us to compromise, to believe this is all life has to offer.

I've been in this place myself. However, I've experienced and observed that our dreams of sexual desire do exist and can be experienced, to the delight of all involved.

The more comfortable we are about allowing the strangeness of erotic experiences, based on the trust and support provided within a relationship which honors our lovers, the more desired experiences we can achieve for our relationship. The word "more" is the key. Instead of confining your life, by living behind false understands, which create an environment in which lovemaking just gets less, let your guard down. Learn to enjoy your lover, honor your lover, and support your lover. Share who you really want to be with your lover in order to taste the limitless possibilities of life.

I recall a cable television program about a brothel in Nevada. The owner had been in a relationship with a very attractive employee, who was portrayed as being not only a successful employee there, but also a successful actress in the adult entertainment business. It appeared the women who work in this type of business could separate animal sexual instinct and their jobs from their personal love lives.

However, the owner of the brothel was sexual with anyone, including other employees of his establishment, on a consistent basis. From what I could tell, he was honest about it and seemed to treat people, the ladies, with respect. Yet, over time, the woman he was in a relationship with began to be jealous. She reached the point where she could no longer continue working for the man and his establishment, nor remain in an intimate relationship with him under such terms.

In this particular program's episode, the woman was coming for a visit, having been gone from the brothel for two years. Her arrival and visit were documented. She explained she was now a strong woman and no one would ever control her again. She said she felt the owner of the brothel was a nice man, but a man with a need to control people. She appeared uncomfortable and not at all confident about the visit, despite her efforts to portray just the opposite.

I'm not going to make judgments about legal brothels or their moral values or peoples' desired experiences. I want only to share my observations about this situation.

First, relationships can very seldom be sexually intimate and not produce a desire for love, over time. Love is very different than sex. You would think a successful, professional, sex entertainer could separate the two in her life. However, once love and the desire to be unique and special entered into the relationship, at least on her part, what she desired from the relationship changed drastically.

Expectations of her inner, most desired, experiences quickly overpowered her intellectual ability to justify a situation she found unacceptable for achieving the desires of her existence. Confusion lingered, regarding what choices were best for her. This is proven by her justification for behaviors that wouldn't allow her to feel what she actually wanted and by her relative discomfort in returning to a place where she experienced some type of loss. She wasn't sure if her choices were best for her or not.

Second, the understanding the lady took away from this experience taught her to protect herself from the exact thing she desired.

It was obvious she was uncomfortable, felt shamed or used in some manner. Why else would she stress that she would never let someone control her again, as the brothel owner had done? Being hurt or shamed isn't about doing something we don't want to do. Most humans find it easy to say no to things they don't want. Being hurt or shamed is about not being able to experience something we want to experience. We find it difficult to look bad to others, when it appears we let someone do something to us, something we wanted, which eventually caused us pain or distress, due to the situation.

Of course, we can't admit it was our choice to be included in the experience in the first place. That would mean we wanted it! The lady learned a behavior, to never be controlled by anyone again. This is just another cliché we hold on to and use when we really have no idea of what's going on or what we need to do to produce our desires. She likely has no idea what she was really trying to portray, when she communicated this message about her new behavior. She learned, sadly, to protect herself from needing to feel the way she wanted to feel in the situation to start with. She wanted this man to commit to her and belong to her. Any fool could see this. Why else had she needed to leave, unable to bear his continued sexual behaviors with all the other women?

As a professional sexual entertainer, she has sex with all sorts of men. However, in return for her surrender to his control, she desired him to forsake all others, or at least limit himself, in this case. She will always desire to surrender, as its part of woman's nature, but this experience taught her that she can't allow herself to be in this situation again, in order to avoid being hurt or shamed. It's not the nature of her desire to surrender that produced the undesired results for her. It was the choice she made that produced the confusion, allowing herself to think her desires could be achieved in this situation. She put herself with the wrong guy and in the wrong job to get what she dearly desired, proof of her worthiness of devoted love.

Third, love is not sex. Even the brothel owner explained that if you want to be a good lover, you must understand the person, as well as sexual techniques and the body. This I've experienced. Good, actually amazing, sexual experiences come from understanding the laws of the human spirit, not the laws of the human body. Although pleasure is and can be induced by the body, it's not enough to make the experience of love grow over time. Creating an environment for the growth of sexual experiences requires much more. We must know who we are in gender, allow someone to know us, and our efforts to participate in and support the desires of our partners, are all necessary components for sex to be experienced as deep connection of love. We need the understanding of pleasure and open honesty and trust. Sex can be good – really good – to start with, but if you want it to last and get even better, you'll need to jump from new experiences of continually different partners, because eventually a deeper desire of love will change the experience.

Fourth, sex is more than an instinctual urge to procreate the species. It's an act of deep possibilities for the expression of our existence. When sex is performed as a behavior for loving and pleasing, the boundaries are stripped away and the intensity of connection for our souls with another becomes unlimited. It just keeps getting better.

In light of these observations, could a situation, such as that involving the brothel owner, work for achieving a person's desires? Remember, the universe contains the infinite and all situations and solutions have possibilities. In fact, you can see proof of the possible attainment of a person's desires in this particular scenario.

The male owner of the brothel was getting love from all sorts of women. This love was sufficient enough so that he didn't have to commit himself to one person, yet his dreams of loving connections as intimate as can be possible were all being met. Granted, this situation was very one sided and some people were getting hurt. However, if he was making choices that were best for him, allowing him to achieve his desires, and if he wasn't being false with others and was behaving truthfully, with desires to hurt no one, then it's up to the one feeling hurt and shamed to learn to make the choices that are best for them. Don't think you can change someone to fit your life. Find people who are what you want and who are willing to understand and take into consideration what you desire from life.

The specifics of sex for each relationship will be what that relationship desires. We all have differences. Learning how to be cognizant of our partner's specific buttons is as simple as listening to the reactions created by our touch. Our physical, emotional and mental touches produce our spiritual touch. This is the touch we need to use, to understand someone else's pleasurable desires.

Sex is a place to share each other, a place where the vessel can splash a bit of itself into another. Imagine you're looking down at the open top of two full glasses of water. Put them as close together as you can, so they're touching. Rock them back and forth against each other, just enough to let some of the water spill out of each glass, over into the adjoining glass.

This is the idea of sex and how joining together allows for the possibility of touch and/or sharing our souls.

Now, imagine the vessels, glasses themselves, are uniquely shaped for each sex to fit together and perform the same experiment for this experience. I've included simple diagrams for visualization of this concept. They show how nature has provided for a way for souls to better come together in this universe.

Each of these ideas of sexual behavior allows for the sharing of the soul. One obviously allows for a much deeper and abundant sharing than the others. Again, this isn't meant to be literal. It's a conceptual representation of the idea of sexual behaviors.

I'm not an advocate or proponent of any particular preference in life style or sexual choices. These are individual preferences and experiences that only the people involved in can define as being best for them.

MALE

FEMALE

HETEROSEXUAL SEX

FEMALE HOMOSEXUAL SEX

MALE HOMOSEXUAL SEX

CHAPTER TWENTY NINE

STANDARDS AND EXPECTATIONS

THIS IS A TOUGH subject, because of its duality. Most religious and physical health specialists talk about balance, about being on the straight and narrow path. Understanding this is often difficult, as balance requires looking at both the need for something and abstinence from the same thing. We need to have the control to enjoy the excesses of our existence, as well as knowing when to refrain from them.

Standards and expectations are a balance, one that gets in the way of our happiness, as well as being necessary for it.

Accepting that someone who beats you actually loves you and willingly accepting this abuse for any reason is not a good thing. Expecting people in your life to be productive and put forth an effort for a better life is a reasonable expectation. Placing strict rules on whether someone you want in your life should have a college education, make a certain amount of money or look a specific way only hinders you from having an open mind to a possibility that could become exactly what you desire to experience.

Most expectations or standards are judgments. Yes, we are human and humans make judgments. It's one of our primary instincts, a result of our need to look good, as well as survive. Once again, we're doing what others tell us we should do, in order to conform.

We're often left to compromise on the expectations we desire from life. The rules we grab onto keep us from experiencing the ultimate life we dream of. I remind you of this, because I'm about to explain a key to providing a place to experience the ultimate life experience. It is within intimate relations.

I've observed that many intimate relations are consummated around rules and expectations that limit the possibility of living a life of great fulfillment. As discussed earlier, we must know who we are and who we want to be and have the ability and courage to articulate these expectations to a mate, in order to eliminate confusion. Many of life's deepest desires are within intimate relations, yet we set rules that hinder ever experiencing some of our deepest desires, fantasies if you wish, especially in monogamous, life-long commitments. This only sets us up for disappointments and produces feelings of regret that we aren't experiencing what we know and dream life can be.

There is almost no reason for not finding a way to provide a place within an intimate relationship, where all a mate's desires can be experienced, from simple ideas of house and home to erotic intimacy. If a mate desires to be a sportsman, we should provide a safe and supportive place in our lives for his or her interest. If a mate wishes to enjoy an erotic, sensual experience, we should be open to supporting such a desire. If you mate for life, there's no other honorable place to go to achieve one's life desires. To set rules and/or expectations that hinders the possibility of achieving a life fantasy or dream will likely lead to discontentment and sets limitations on the possibilities of a relationship.

Obviously, there need to be considerations on both sides of the relationship. It wouldn't be wise for a provider and head of a family to take up a life-threatening activity, especially if both parties have agreed in advance that this type of risk is an undesired expectation, which could jeopardize the survival of the family. However, if you knew, before any commitments were made, that your mate wanted to live a risky life and you agreed to that possibility, then you should be as supportive as possible, even though you have real and truthful fears of loss. Our dreams are what can make us the best of who we are and being loved for who we are is the only true love there is.

My wife has a saying regarding a loved one to whom you want to be married. "You must love all of the person, not just the filling, but the crust also."

What she means is that having a resentment free relation requires you to want all of a person, not just that which will make you look good. You must trust and experience all that each other desires and provide the opportunities for the experiences each desire. There is no other place for a person to go to for these experiences, without dishonoring someone.

Some things may take time to get used to. It may be necessary to gain an understanding of something, before you can be open to it. The point is, putting a rule in front of it will only produce the possibility of a desire never being a possibility.

Play. Experiment. Experience. This is the only way to truthfully know if you can accept an idea or desire, maybe even enjoy it. With this type of open-minded relationship, you'll find that when something is just too hard for you to accept, this will be understood and not resented, because of all the other possibilities remaining to choose from.

This idea is particularly important when it comes to intimacy within a committed relationship. If you've given your word to be monogamous and promised not to pursue possibilities or intimate or erotic experiences with anyone else, the only place such desires can be honorably experienced is within the committed relationship.

Love is about being, providing and feeling you're in a safe forum with your lover and able to be what you desire to be. When we restrict the desires of our loved ones, we send a message that our love has a condition. This can easily produce a behavior to protect ourselves from consequences of that condition.

One of the most common protective behaviors in this situation is resistance to open dialogue about important issues, our innermost, important truths and desires. While in most cases there isn't a conscious decision to behave this way, we fear that something we desire to experience in our lives can disappear and the safe place in which we desire to exist starts to disappear, leaving us unable to express who and what we want to be. Fear motivated behaviors have a strong possibility of producing reactive fear motivated behaviors. Fear and reaction to fear can easily begin a cycle of behaviors that don't produce a desired outcome.

Perfection, especially from humans, is not a reality. The ability to understand and deal graciously with imperfection is a necessary tool, if any relationship is going to include unlimited possibilities to be all that is desired. Judging and blaming others for their inability to live up to our thoughts of how something should exist only starts a cycle of resentment. No one appreciates having their faults and failures waved in their face. Usually, we've berated ourselves more than enough for our mistakes. If you wish to see something good come from someone else's mistakes, show them you love them, even when you're embarrassed by their mistakes. Trust them to learn from the mistake and move on to what's next.

As is true in many circumstances and situations, we only limit our happiness by holding on to the understandings of intimate relationships we've been taught. Like sex or lovemaking, let your experiences with a trusted lover be what is real and not what someone has told you it should be.

In addition to refusing to be bound by rules that will prevent us enjoying possible experiences we desire from life, we must also know how to communicate our expectations and have the courage to do so. We must understand others don't know or understand what we desire and stop believing others should be able to figure us out.

If we can't define our expectations and standards for ourselves, how can we explain ourselves to others? If we don't explain our expectations and standards, how will others know how to behave? How will they know the best way to honor us or if what we desire for ourselves is possible for them to live with?

Most arguments are due to the lack of understanding of someone's expectations and not the subject of conflict. Few people have the courage to communicate expectations, because of the possible consequences of such conversations. Just as our employer may not agree with our expectations and, therefore, not desire us as an employee, so our lover may not agree with our expectations and not want us as a lover.

This becomes even more critical, once we have commitments or investments in someone or something. If we commit to a relationship, before communicating expectations, and the relationship starts to have issues and problems, the need to communicate those expectations is going to be necessary to help the relationship continue on a desired course. However, it also provides the possibility of destroying the relationship.

This produces behaviors of denial and avoidance. We fear that if we show our truths, we'll lose something we desire. We often argue and become demanding about unimportant issues and small things in our lives, hoping this will produce some proof that someone cares enough about who we are to understand us and consider what's important to us.

We need standards and expectations, but only to the point where they protect us from possible injury, loss or pain. We don't need them to make us look good to someone who has defined their own rules for what looking good means.

We must have the courage and intelligence to communicate what is important in our lives and how we feel our lives should exist. Without this, we waste time and efforts, suffering under the delusion the world should be able to figure out who we desire to be and what's important to our existence.

It's important to take responsibility for understanding how our standards can get in our way. I remember talking with a lady when I was dating and between relationships. She complained that she thought she wasn't good-looking enough to attract the love she desired in her life. I explained to her she could find love at just about any minute. I offered to take her out on the town and find someone who would want to love her and be kind to her.

She told me she couldn't accept just anyone, that she needed certain qualities from a lover. At that point, I told her she needed to stop complaining and realize her standards were getting in the way of her possible happiness. She needed to take responsibility for her standards.

Standards do get in our way, even if they are important to our lives. We need to realize this and take responsibility for ways in which our standards can get in the way of obtaining certain desired experiences.

I've observed that few relations, that turn into committed relations, that the expectations of the persons in the relationship have been discussed. I've also observed that many long lasting relationships often come from persons with active religious cultures. I believe this is due to either a process for communicating expectations for a relationship or a taught, common understanding of expectations of a relationship.

Most relationships, in which expectations haven't been shared and in which problems later arise, have a commonality. The problems mostly center around arguments that the people in the relationship don't feel understood by each other. Some small issue, which could be easily resolved, turns into testing and posturing by one party or the other, maintaining the other person doesn't pay attention to his or her rules for how someone who loves them should treat them.

Much of the confusion in relationships can be eliminated. By knowing your expectations, by communicating them, and by not using them as a tool to test how much someone loves you. Stick to the issues, when dealing with disagreements, as they can be difficult enough as it is. Select another time and forum to deal with your expectations of life and people.

Compared to other intimate relationships I've had, my wife and I have very few arguments. Most arguments are about a very few subjects that are difficult for us to resolve, due to circumstances beyond our influences. We're human. We don't always agree on subjects and we do argue. Many of our behaviors are not completely the way the other person thinks is the best behavior in the world.

However, because we discussed what's important to us, and who we desire to be, before we walked down the aisle of matrimony, we accept and dearly love the other for who they are and want to be. We also know when we aren't living up to the other's expectations, and it's easy to not become defensive when the other person may express a desire that's not understood or fulfilled. We don't judge each other's desires. We truly feel it's our responsibility to find ways to support the other's desires, even when it's not easy or not a part of our desired choices for a behavior.

Chapter Thirty

GENDER

THE LAW OF GENDER says we are male, female or not. We are male, female, asexual or a form of mutation which is an anomaly. If you are male or female, I doubt you're asexual and the percentage of anomalies is so small, until we learn how to change the genetics of our cells and/or transplant sexual organs and glands, we're what we're born as, a man or a woman.

So much of the world defines for us the acceptable manners for our behaviors, for us to appear wise and having some value, we've lost, or are losing, the essential differences which are a natural part of making the opposite sexes happy.

Women aren't allowed to appear needy. Men have to be sensitive. It's not a question of whether this has any specific truth, it's just an example of rules being defined. Constant change is the only consistent rule about rules. Rules are made up and followed, believed to be beneficial to the sexes, even though no proof exists about the extent of liberation of the sexes.

Let's be honest. The advances in rights and equality in the world have obviously improved the quality of living for all, but how has the abandonment of true differences between the sexes affected happy relationships? I'm not going to say I have concrete knowledge about the results, but I am going to state my opinion, based on what I've experienced and observed.

When it comes to our interactions with the world, the idea of equality is just right. However, when you enter a committed, heterosexual relationship, the idea of equality is just false.

Men and women are different. Defining the behaviors acceptable for each sex, based on survival and protection, which I observe to be rampant in today's cultures, is a failure to care for the desires of our existence. Women have unique qualities of beauty and intuition, with desires to be cared for in specific manners. Men have unique qualities of strength and focus, to accomplish objectives.

I know many of you are going to complain that I'm just another source for yet another definition of what each sex desires and these definitions don't reflect your true nature. These ideas are archaic, chauvinistic and anti-feminist.

I don't care. What's true is true. Although I find these ideas of feminism and male sensitivity nothing more than clichés, I'm looking for answers that produce happiness, not answers to fairness or equality or survival. This work has already been done and done to the point of going too far. I'm being very general with any definitions on purpose. I understand there are unique points of view and desires and exceptions to all understandings.

The necessities of survival demand that specific behaviors can be much more productive. Women may need to be stronger than their nature desires and men may need to be more sensitive than their natures desire, in order to achieve greater goals. This should be understood and is not a failure for achieving the desires of the soul. However, if there is no place that provides the ability for the nature of our souls, as differing sexes, to exist and if we're not willing to create such a place, we are only surviving and not experiencing the dreams of existence. By letting the survival behaviors of our existence be a priority for all aspects of existence, we fail to allow the nature of our differences to produce all that is possible for the attainment of our desired experiences.

To negatively judge the honest, useful exploitation of the difference in our natures, the differences between the two sexes, is a failure to recognize our desires. Using any unique qualities you have for honest advantage is what life should be and is all about. A woman who can use her charms and unique natures as a woman to excel in her business, as well as in her personal life, is only fulfilling her natural desires. A man who uses his focus and strength to do the same thing is only fulfilling his natural desires.

To be blunt, when it comes to the bottom line, a woman wants to surrender to life and have it serve her and a man desires to serve life and be appreciated and honored for his efforts. I've observed that when I find opposition to this understanding, it's the result of some type of taught experience. That experience has produced a need to protect the nature of who we are, as differing sexes, in order to survive the confusion about our souls' desires or to look good to the world around us. The fear someone will discover we want a differently understood experience of existence, rather than what has been taught to us as acceptable and normal, is the influence for this point of view.

Women today are a good example of the need to protect ourselves from our nature. Experiences often teach women that surrendering to anyone or anything will get them hurt. This creates a hesitancy, which is justifiable, but no justification negates the truth that hiding our nature behind protective behaviors puts enormous limits on our desired experiences.

A woman, who was sexually molested, as a child or an adult, may never allow herself to trust anybody enough to allow herself any place in her existence to surrender and be served. A man who's been ridiculed for his desires and character may never trust that his existence has any value, that he deserves to be desired and honored by anyone, much less the opposite sex. Both of these scenarios produce behaviors to find ways to survive life, rather than behaviors that allow us to experience life's desires for our natures.

I observe it is possible to uncover the basic desires for our nature, as a given sex, in anyone, no matter how deep their nature is being hidden and protected from the world. It may appear in a simple statement. "Well, sure, I'd love it to be that way, if only it was a possibility, but life isn't that idealistic and I want to survive."

Few of us get the chance to actually experience something that shows us our true dreams for our existence are even possible. This is sad. In truth, we can change our point of view and make the world be what we desire it to be, no matter what our existence and experiences have shown us is or is not possible to this point.

This nature is part of us, whether we are gay, flaming, lesbian, butch or just masculine and feminine. I've found no exceptions, although I've never really known a true hermaphrodite. I admit exceptions can and do exist and a true hermaphrodite may be such an exception, but our natures are not a matter of mannerisms or specific traits of character. Our nature is our nature. Thus, the "Law of Gender."

Whether a woman uses her natural desires in business and out in the world or behaves in manners at odds with her nature, as a woman isn't the issue. The issues is, somewhere in her life, she needs a place to experience her nature, at home or in a relationship, in order to experience her desires in full. The same is true for a man, who needs someplace to experience his own nature, to fulfill his deepest desires.

It's obvious it may be very difficult for some of us to have a place, which allows for the experiences of the nature of our gender. A single mother may have no place or no one to surrender to and must spend her efforts just making a living for her family. A bachelor may have no one to serve and no one to value his efforts. However, there are many possible places to provide us with an opportunity to experience the differing natures of our sex. Only our imaginations limit us to these possibilities for experiencing our desires.

There is no justification for believing we have to provide the world an understanding or explanation for where it is we find the place to experience our desires. In fact, justification of this goes directly against our nature. It is a personal issue for each of us. Each of us must find a place that allows us to fulfill our natures.

We should also keep in mind that the basic forms of life, such as single-celled organisms, do not depend on sexes to survive. Even the cells in our own bodies multiply on their own. Somewhere in the process of evolution or creation, the more advanced organisms separated, taking some pieces of the existence of our beings to one sex and others to the opposite sex. This leads to the logical conclusion that each sex is lacking in some feature of existence in this universe.

This conclusion says we are different in some way and these differences leave us with natures unique to each sex. Knowledge is one of life's rewards for life's experience. The knowledge gained from the ability to understand the opposite sex, the differences in our two natures, is one of great rewards. It allows us the possibility to regain the union of one, which was separated to produce the two different sexes. This understanding and manifestation of the union of the sexes, we call sex and lovemaking. We'll discuss this union in more detail, because of its ability to provide desired experiences beyond the singular, unique experiences of our individuality.

While understanding our own nature is not a matter to be considered lightly or useless, it is easier than gaining an understanding of something that is different from our own nature. Understanding another, different, point of view is more difficult and brings greater rewards.

I was impressed by the proclamation of truth I heard from a transsexual, who was being interviewed during a hidden camera reality show on cable television. It seemed very healthy and showed this person was at peace with making the choice to experience his life as a transsexual.

He explained that no matter what he'd done and gone through, he could never really experience life as a woman and he is still, and always will be, a man. His genes can't be changed. He can never bear a child, have a menstrual cycle nor know how a woman's sexual sensations, responses, orgasms or genitals truthfully feel. However, the choice he made for the experiences he desires is one that is his right to make and experience. He loves his way of life and has no reason to falsify the truth, in order to justify his choice and be accepted for it.

CHAPTER THIRTY ONE

MAKING LOVE

I'M GOING TO SHARE with you some basic understandings of what makes sexual relations move to a behavior of lovemaking, versus just sex. Erotic sexual experiences are often thought of as a mythical, unrealistic fantasy for many people and are real for only a few of us.

The inability to lose limitations and remove inhibitions for the sexual expressions of love produces a society of doubters, a majority of sexually unsatisfied people. Because sex and love have been disappointing experiences for them, they conclude real, erotic, fulfilling sexuality is nothing more than a rumor and live life accordingly.

To enjoy the erotic sexual experiences most people only dream of, an open level of trust or faith is necessary. This allows us to let go of our concerns about the possibilities of negative experiences. We need to trust and believe that deep, unlimited possibilities, the infinite, exists with sexual experiences, as it does with all other aspects of our existence, that this is as real as every other possibility of the infinite.

We need to free our minds of intellectual clutter. Such clutter gets in the way of the spiritual pathways, which allow sex to be an expression of love the soul uses as a tool to communicate with and touch another soul. Using the intellect to justify our ability to rationalize the sexual experiences as disappointing is only one choice. We can choose to experience erotic sexuality as a limitless, joyful experience.

Sex is not rational. Sex is stripping down our relative existence as far as possible, to experience something beyond the physical alone.

If you really want sex to become satisfying and erotic lovemaking, your mind must not be running the experience. All intellectual judgments of relative value and quality must be released. All fear of displeasure must be removed from our expectations. All judgment about mistakes must only be present for the moment necessary to communicate a tolerance threshold to our partners or ourselves in an accepting, loving, nonjudgmental manner, without retained resentment.

Acceptance of each other's desire to understand and discover our lover's desires must be an inarguable choice as an unalienable truth. We must take the responsibility for our choices. If we choose to see making love as conditional, we're easily limiting possibilities. If we choose to see making love as an intensely desirable experience for discovering possibilities, we allow for unlimited fulfillment.

You have to want it and go after it. Discover what works for you and your partner. Trust in it and practice it, without judging its purpose, meaning or value.

Our soul uses the mind and intellect to achieve its desires. Only the mind is capable of either limiting love or getting out of the way, for our souls to experience love.

When we decide to let our minds tell us what is acceptable versus disrespectful, we hide our truth. To find the truth about the unlimited pleasures of making love, we must let what sensitivity exists for our being – physical, spiritual, emotional, intellectual and desirable – be discovered, stimulated and enjoyed, through creatively playful experiences.

Remember, pleasure is the point between sensation and pain. If it's easily hurt, it's most likely a place of possible extreme pleasure. Take it slow and careful and, with a little less stimulation, you'll find it feels amazing to be stimulated.

I've observed the heterosexual male's knowledge, understanding and proficiency for providing a woman the necessary contributions for a thriving, pleasurable sexual experience is uncommon. I would say the same of the female gender. Our environments have provided few sources or examples that are consistently credible to produce confident trust in the reality of sexual attainment. You may hear wild possibilities but, if you never experience anything remotely close to the fulfillment of proclaimed sexual declarations or desired sexual experiences, you live in disbelieve of any possible truthful alternatives.

It's difficult to convince anyone of the aspects of any truth that requires a change in their consistently supported point of few. Once we've found something uncomfortable, we rarely return to that feeling to discover other possibilities or truths. However, the truth is that the most uncomfortable actions can turn into the most fulfilling actions. Through open experimentation, my wife and I have produced ongoing and constantly recurring orgasms, resulting in a euphoria we can only define as experiencing a place of nirvana. The feeling of being one with each other has been achieved and surpassed. We've both been blown away by our souls experiencing more than our wildest expectations.

Serve your lover, by exploring their desires wantonly. Give yourself to the moment completely. Let the thoughts of what you're experiencing focus only on the feeling of being stimulated. Discover what you experience, when you provide stimulation. Let the pleasure be communicated by both as acts of love.

While you need to be intelligent about your behaviors, letting go of consequences for sexual experiences is the only way to clear your mind and relax. This is why monogamy, the ability to trust and make a commitment, can produce greater possibilities. When we have no reason to consider the dangers of disease, for example, and trust we'll be supported and united through any consequences, such as pregnancy, fears of possible undesired consequences are removed. When we are familiar with the specific desires and thresholds of our lovers, it provides the open path for souls to touch, by removing intellectually stimulated hesitations or restrictions. Only when we decide not to care about the consequences or remove the fear of any consequences for our sexual experiences are our souls given the freedom to find each other.

If we think about the possibility of an undesired pregnancy while making love, our energy and thoughts are focused on the techniques for birth control. Thoughts restrict the soul's access to the physical experience. The soul communicates through the mind and intellect and experiences through the sensations of naturally achieved experiences. When our minds are cluttered with the task of processing any information, other than the experience of the moment, the moment is cheated of our energy and attention.

When we put a thought in the path of the soul, we block our soul from communicating its moment to experience existence in this universe. We also limit the moment, by choosing to consider restrictions for our desires. This produces tension from conclusions that intellectual control is necessary for the physical, sexual experience to not produce undesirable consequences.

When the intellect is in control the energy of the soul doesn't get to express itself, through the fulfillment of a satisfaction of an accomplished desired experience, which produces the proof that produces the confidence, which comes from the successful manifestation of desires. Open abandonment to the moment also provides the soulful energy of our truths, which is shared and expressed only in the act of sexual love. The soul doesn't get to experience the physical pleasures of being the influence to guide the body to be stimulated with the energy being directed from and wantonly shared by a lover's attainable pleasure of the moment when the intellect is in its way. Open intellectual abandonment and abandonment of consequential concerns provides a lover's soul the opportunity to guide and influence the physical stimulations of their body, allowing for the joining of life to naturally build physical stimulation to moments of complete abandonment of any conscious realization or awareness of the existence of individuality.

The intellect will try to reason understandings for the aspects of sexuality. This produces false conclusions that influence our choices about the way we allow ourselves to experience aspects of sexual intimacy. You cannot rationalize an understanding of the human desire to experience pleasure, but you can produce experiences, which allow for un-imagined pleasurable sensations. It starts with desires to discover the possibilities of attainable experiences. This is not just a willingness to be open to discovery, but a craving to motivate the creation of effort to discover possibility.

Letting go affects the spirit, as well as the body. If we tense up from an active mind, one consumed with worry over all the issues and consequences of a sexual experience, the body won't be aroused to produce desire and won't open up from the expectation of possible manifestation for desired experiences. Coital penetration will be experienced with caution and fear of discomfort. If you truly want to allow for no limitations, a woman should want nothing other than feeling the seed of her lover being abandoned to her body. She should actively behave to acquire it, strive to get it. She must mentally think of nothing more than achieving her lover's climax. In so doing, she finds her own unlimited climaxes, by focusing her thoughts and energies on what is making her feel pleasure, rather than on the consequences of her pleasure.

CHAPTER THIRTY TWO

LOVE

I'VE EXPLAINED THAT LOVE is one element of happiness. Love may involve a spouse, parents, siblings, family, constituents and even self. Some are stronger than others. I know many will argue family love or love between a parent and a child can be the strongest, but my observations show spousal love is the strongest of all.

Although spousal love is not a necessity and the love between children and parents has a unique bond and strength, spousal love is a more difficult love to master and apply to our lives. When applied successfully, it is the love that guides parental love to an even greater experience. Spousal love is where sexual intimacy should take place. Even our love for our creator can't provide sexual, intimate connections of the physical and spiritual. Nonetheless, spousal love is only one place where love can be found and isn't necessary for happiness. Sufficient love can be found in many other forums.

When it comes to love, it's not as simple as saying we love one thing more than another. While that may be true in some cases, it's often a matter of loving some things differently.

I love and treat my wife differently than my children, but one doesn't come before the other. I don't love one more than the other, I love them differently. My wife doesn't need me to be a father to her. She needs me to be a husband and a partner. I expect my wife to understand the time I must spend doing things that aren't about her. If she becomes jealous, when my time is spent on or with things other than her, I expect her to deal with the feeling with respect and maturity. I would have less patience with her annoying behaviors than with those of my children.

If my children become annoying, perhaps interrupting and demanding my attention when I'm busy, I'll be more patient about explaining and, perhaps, adjusting the situation, than I would be with my wife. In a similar vein, a younger child wouldn't be scolded for making the same mess as an older child. The older youngster has the knowledge and ability to take responsibility for messes he or she makes.

As to love in and of its self, I've observed that understanding we're in love, or that we love someone or something, is something we're all able to do pretty simply. This doesn't mean we know how to make the best choices about love.

We need to be able to define the differences between love and other aspects of our existence, in order to make informed choices about how to deal with our lives, when we desire to experience love. The key here is having some sort of definition, which allows us a foundation for informed decision making. Below is my definition of love. It works for me and I hope, at least in some part, it will work for you.

Love:
The adoration we have for someone we find unique and who finds us unique.
Un-acquired Love:
The adoration we have for someone we find unique and whom we wish found us unique.

Many of you may find these definitions hard to agree with. I'll discuss them in more detail later. For now, understand that if you're asked, "Are you in love?" you won't be able to answer the question with confidence and without confusion, unless you have a stable, non-transient definition of love. Having a definition that fits your desires is of grave importance.

CHAPTER THIRTY THREE

UNCONDITIONAL LOVE

L OVING UNCONDITIONALLY IS A powerful tool for our happiness. When we put conditions on our love for people who depend on our love for their happiness, they fear they'll lose a precious experience, unless they live up to all the known and unknown conditions. When humans fear loss, we produce behaviors to protect ourselves from the pain of that loss or possible loss. Most of these protective behaviors against the loss of love are adverse to the support of love. Most people will find ways to remove their love, before love is removed from them.

Unconditional love is when we choose to love someone for who they are, including their faults and our faults in judging who we think they should be. When we choose to love someone unconditionally, we must be responsible for our choice and not put conditions on other people to insure our happiness.

Do you want someone to tell you what you must do or how you must change, in order for him or her to love you? This type of behavior from people we hardly know is usually rejected and we won't accept it. However, this type of behavior from someone with whom we have a history and to whom we've made commitments is destructive to all aspects of a relationship.

People who must live up to conditions will have fears of loss and engage in unproductive behaviors to protect themselves. Over time, resentment builds up, because they don't feel loved for who they are, nor do they feel they're being honored with the promises of love that were given to them. Obviously, no small issue.

The people mandating the conditions for love have issues they need to deal with. Most of these conditions for love are habitually taught desires and behaviors, which have little to do with providing them their desired experiences. They also have to deal with the unproductive behaviors their conditions bring forth and the confusion these behaviors cause them. High on the list of the unproductive behaviors is the fact that the other person will begin holding back love and placing their own conditions on returning love.

We don't stop loving a child because of his or her mistakes. Good parents know how to love unconditionally. However, as children grow up, it's common for people to start putting conditions on them, usually not very realistic ones or conditions observed as truthful. A lot of parents put conditions on their younger children, too. This results in our children believing love must be earned and not given and respected, because we're not willing to take responsibility for our choices. This is when we begin absorbing learned behaviors. I can only love you, like you or be your friend based on a set of conditions I don't understand, but which someone told me were necessary.

We don't have to agree with or support unacceptable or false behaviors, but neither do we have to take away our love, once we've committed it, because we don't have the ability to deal with our choice. We can disagree, have differences and expectations, without putting conditions on the people we love, which will make them feel they must change to meet our desires or they'll no longer be worthy of our love.

Unconditional love is almost impossible. Even if we can love unconditionally, that doesn't mean relationships are unconditional. Our standards and desired qualities for our lives get in the way. However, we can have expectations and standards, without asking our loved ones to change the aspects or principles of who they desire to be. We need to remember their uniqueness is what we fell in love with in the first place. Asking them to conform to our personal ideals for ourselves is not a productive behavior. Asking a loved one to change, in order for us to look good to the world, is never going to produce the relationships we desire.

We need to support the desires and uniqueness of the people we love. We need to provide guidance to being happy and healthy, not try to control them through requiring them to conform to our demands. The only conditions we should put on our love are the ones we discuss and agree to or ones that protect us from being selfishly harmed by others, when it comes to the relationship.

CHAPTER THIRTY FOUR

RELATIONSHIPS

COMPLICATED AND STRESSFUL RELATIONSHIPS can make or break us in so many ways. Before we can even consider addressing the issues of our relationships, we must first deal with the issue of ourselves. This is why I've been going over the best ways to determine how to live your desires and not the best way to convince someone else to be your desires, although living your desires is the best way to find someone you desire.

We often find ourselves in discussions about others rather than considering ourselves, when we're dealing with relationship issues, and we often prefer to point blame at someone other than ourselves. We demand they be the ones to change or do something, in order for us to be happy within our relationships. In truth, we're the ones with the power and influence to make our relationships work and this has little to do with others. Whether it's a choice of who to be with or how to create the place we wish to be in, as in creating moments of complete joy, the power to produce the experiences we desire with other people lies within our own efforts.

We must have the ability to provide others a place to be, before a relationship can produce the dream we desire. We must love people for who they are, not for what we want them to be.

If our partners aren't living their dream, due to either their issues of confusion or our behaviors, they will produce negative behaviors, to protect them from their fears of either not living the dream or losing it. These behaviors are their response to the possibility of shattered dreams.

We must begin with ourselves. Learn what it means to love unconditionally and how to do so. Be sure of who you want to be and who you want to be with, as well as who you are and who you will not be. Have the courage and ability to communicate your expectations.

Don't try to change someone to fit your desires. Love them and show them they're safe to observe the truths in their lives, within this relationship, so they can let go and love in return, while learning and knowing, through experience and example, the dream does exist. All we have to do is have the courage and maturity to live it.

When we feel honored for who we are, it's much easier to honor and be attentive to someone else's desires. We must build the house in which we wish to live.

If you're a slob, it doesn't matter how neat the person you're with may be. You'll mess up the house and, eventually, the person who's always cleaning it up, because you want a clean house, will resent the work they must do to make you happy. From what I've observed, we all want a clean house. We all want to live the dream that all of our relationship desires are being fulfilled.

No matter how good your partner is, if you don't do the work necessary to produce a place that makes their dreams possible for them, if you don't support their desires, the relationship will have issues you don't desire. You must take responsibility for doing what it takes to make your desires a reality and not make this the responsibility of others. The examples of how we live our lives have the power to influence the people in our lives. Behave as the person you want to be and you'll help others understand how this can benefit them, as well.

Don't let others tell you how to behave or act, in order to get what you desire from a relationship. Let your heart and soul do this. The lessons we've learned from our world so far won't necessarily work for making us happy. Moreover, the lessons we haven't learned, because no one has really known how to teach us, need to be learned, if we desire to live our dreams.

Love is an emotion that can be unconditional. A relationship is a thing that cannot. I can love someone I couldn't live with or agree with on his or her basic principles of existence. Love is somewhat difficult to explain. Why do we feel this way for any given person? To deny it is not a good choice, but to let it control you is equally unwise. I cannot leave out the idea that some basic desires of the soul, for a connection of the soul, exist. In some ways, we can define love, but whom we admire or adore isn't always understandable. This is called desire.

In a relationship, we should consider someone who can and will be good to us. We need someone who has learned what it takes to be good to someone they love, or who is willing to learn. Most of us have no idea how to treat someone we love. The divorce rate is all the proof we need of this lack of understanding. The stubbornness that leads us to believe we need no help to overcome that which we believe we know, which has been taught to us, is relentless.

If you're considering a long term relationship with someone who is unable to admit they're wrong about what they know, I'd bet the relationship is going to fail in some form or produce no joy. I may lose that bet a few times, but the odds that I'm correct are so greatly in my favor, I can deal with a few losses.

I'm more than willing to deal with the few imperfections of a wonderful person, if it means I gain a lifetime of experiences beyond my expectations. If I'm living up to ninety percent of everything I've ever wanted from a relationship, I can willingly accept the ten percent I discover is not desirable and must deal with, so long as it doesn't represent something completely unacceptable in my life.

I want to be clear about my meaning of the word relationship. I'm not discussing sexual experimentation or the Friday night sexual freak fetishes someone may experience or desire to experience. I'm discussing the issue of a long-term commitment to a given way of life, in which we look to mates and partners for important aspects of our lives and with whom we can share our experiences.

I observe relationships, whether spousal, family, friendship or constituencies, provide greater possibilities for us to experience that which we desire in our existence. To relate is to connect, as to be relative is to connect and compare. We live in a relative world. What could be more natural than to relate or connect?

Let's look at some specifics for heterosexual, long-term, committed relationships. We could just say marriage. I'm going to use a few words that will seem a little prehistoric for today's relationships. When I see the truth, I call it as I see it. First is the word, "master," second is the word, "servant," and third is the word, "subservient." I'd prefer sub-servant, because the true definition of subservient isn't exactly what I mean. I mean "to surrender," rather than to be submissive.

Now, if any of you think either party or sex can be the master of a relationship, you're just fooling yourself. You can no more be the master of a relationship than you can cause a law of physics to change or be created. The master of the relationship is the relationship. A relationship has principles you need to understand, just like the laws of physics.

For a relationship to work and produce true happiness for all parties, it must be honored, respected, attended to and prioritized. Remember, we're talking about adult, heterosexual, committed relationships, not friendships or casual sex. Relating to others in small moments of experiences is a different subject than long-term, committed relationships, although everything I'm discussing can relate to any type of relationship.

A committed, monogamous relationship may not be the number one priority in someone's life, but all parties must agree to what priorities are acceptable. I have yet to observe a successful marriage, where the relationship is not put first. Most relationships that can work, without it being the first priority, are not intimate, committed ones.

Respect is important in relationships and life. Being respectful to relationships requires that you discuss your expectations and agree on how to deal with them. Respect asks for maturity. It asks that you don't assume you know what your partner wants from life. Discuss what they want with them. Reading a partner's mind isn't currently a reality, at least in my experience.

Honoring your mate is important and honoring your mate when they're not there is critical. This means you're to treat your mate with respect. It also means you don't allow others to disrespect your mate, whether you're out together or you're out and about in the world without them. You never have to lie for a partner. I recommend you never lie for them or anyone. You should always speak your truth and keep your relationship issues within your relationship. Always give your partner and yourself the respect of honoring him or her and your choice of this mate. Should it become necessary to seek outside support, this can be done in a respectful way, with honor towards each other.

Pay attention to the ones you love. There are many important aspects to a happy relationship. Anything either of you discover that's important to you should be discussed and agreement reached on how to attain what's desired.

There are some basic principles of the master of the relationship, which is the relationship itself.

Servant is the masculine role in a relationship, service to the relationship. This includes service to all the parties involved, including your spouse, your children, yourself and extended members. The masculine role is to maintain the direction and focus of the relationship, to command and consider all other needs, besides its own. The word servant, meaning to serve, is defined as "to satisfy."

Don't think having command and control provides you unconditional power. In truth, in this aspect, it means to command and control in a manner that serves all in the relationship. It means the masculine must consider the other's needs before his own, keep all things safe, teach, mentor and provide good examples of character. It's like a CEO in charge of a corporation, who must think of the corporation's needs over his or her own, at least most of the time.

This is not a directive of what the man or masculine role must be in the world. It's not the necessity of bringing home the bacon, but the necessity to make sure it gets brought home. It doesn't mean the man is more capable or smarter than a woman, the feminine role or his female mate. I'm simply referring to masculine or feminine traits when I use such references as he/she, him/her, man/woman, etc.

I've observed that women contain masterfully high intellects and are much more able to multi-task than men. Women have a general ease and ability for political politeness. However, as I've pointed out, our intellect is not the road to happiness.

A man's ability to focus is his strength for maintaining what is important for producing a healthy relationship and its core purpose is strengthening those within it.

Subservient, or sub-servant, which I shall use, is the female role of the relationship. If you follow the maze of definitions, it will lead you back to the word subservient meaning to surrender and obey. I want to make it clear that the female is not surrendering to a man, but is surrendering to the master, the relationship, and obeying the principles of relationships.

I've tested this and have found women do desire to surrender, to be taken care of, and to have their desires and issues considered voluntarily, sometimes before they recognize they have a desire to be considered.

The idea a woman should surrender to and obey a man is not popular. Neither is the idea that a man must serve a woman. This is why it's critical to understand that neither of these is the case. She is surrendering to the relationship and he is serving it.

Still, the nature of man is to serve and the nature of women is to surrender and this applies to not only the relationship, but to each other. No woman needs to offer the gift of surrender to anyone but her mate. No man has to serve anyone but his partner and family. It's a two way street. If it's going to work and produce respect for each other, both must surrender to their roles and the relationship, which is the master.

A woman's surrender is a gift. A man must serve his lady with the same respect Jesus served the church. A man must give more weight and attention to the considerations, needs and opinions of his family, especially his wife, than he allows for himself. If this isn't the case, it's impossible to create a relationship that grows with time and produces more joy and fulfillment and an admiration for each other which builds over time.

As a man, I'm head of and must serve the relationship, attend to my wife and children, take the lead for the best direction for the family and consider the desires of my wife and family before my own. I must step up and treat the one I love with respect, honor her when she's not there. I need to provide a place for her to be safe, to be who they desire to be, without hiding. I need to allow for mistakes, without fear of losing the relationship.

As a woman, I'm the heart of the relationship and must not only surrender all I am to the relationship, but give wantonly of all I have. I must know my help and opinions are desired, needed and considered by my partner.

These gifts make us feel happy and complete and produce a common, upward lift for the relationship. The heart and the head are both necessary for the body of the relationship to survive. They need each other. Each provides the other what's necessary to survive and without each other, both perish.

I realize I'm discussing a subject and using words that are highly unpopular in today's society. If you observe a true woman's nature, you have a human with two "X" chromosomes. I observe they desire and strive to surrender to existence in some part of their lives. A man must be willing to admit, just as a woman must, that his mate is the most important person in his life and his family comes before himself. If your mate isn't the most important person in your life, why are you in a committed relationship with him or her?

I know many will say blood is thicker than matrimony. However, you didn't choose your blood relations. You did choose your lover. I'd think your choice is more important than your default. I observe when we choose the right person, we will be happier, if we put them first.

It takes two. There's no doubt about this. We can be perfect in our elimination of confusion. We can behave, as we desire to be. Yet, if all parties don't grow towards each other, we may still be in a relationship that doesn't work for us.

Person > Relationship < Person

In the above equation, all are working towards possibility, through support of each other's dreams. This relationship will produce desired experiences for everyone involved.

Person < Relationship < Person

This equation represents the chase, where one person is always chasing the other, looking for proof of love.

Person < Relationship > Person

This shows individuals running away with no support or love for the persons involved.

The last two types of relationships only produce limitations and struggles over time. While there are many types of relationships and various issues within relationships, these simple equations are meant to show it takes all parties of a relationship to support and understand each other, in order for unlimited possibilities for desired experiences to exist.

Discuss your expectations with your chosen lover, long before you get married, make a commitment or move in together.

Communicate your standards and expectations for who you want to be. It's very difficult to use the issue of not being understood, if you've communicated what's important to you and what's unacceptable. It's also easy to catch yourself using issues, which have been previously agreed upon, in ways that don't serve you and produce the person you want to be. Because you can catch yourself, you can stop. It's hard to justify using agreed upon behaviors in ways other than those initially communicated. In addition, you no longer can argue about your agreements, because they were your choice. Yes, things can be adjusted and changed from time to time, but you still need to come to an agreement on standards and expectations.

Relationships are seldom casual for all parties' involved, especially intimate relationships. Usually, one of the persons in the relationship has more invested than the other, whether this is apparent or not. It's possible to have a mutually agreeable casual, intimate relationship, but not probable.

Our relationships with our children are critical to their well-being.

Do not lie to your children. Do not create fantasies that will destroy their trust in you. Lying to our children, in order to produce fantasies for them to experience is truly evil. I'm sorry to say this, because I've observed how much joy, fun and pleasure some fantasies can produce, but this is a short-term result. In the long run, it develops extremely damaging confusion.

Parents are the most trusted people in a child's world. They can do and be no wrong. To discover that parents are not only human and capable of making mistakes, but that they're willing to lie to you about important things in your life, is something children hold on to for a long time. I cannot stress this enough.

We live in societies that enjoy playing with fantasies with our children and our children look to us for the truth of their existences. If your children stop coming to you for your help in their lives, you might want to consider how often you don't provide the truth to them. You can correct this, by talking to them about what you've done and promising to change your behavior.

Relationships are all based in the love of or for something. Love can be given and received in many different forms, as we've discussed. Relationships, of course, come in the same forms. It's easy to find love. It's more important to know how to treat someone you love.

While I'm using and emphasizing spousal intimate relationships for my discussions, there are many types of relations the ideas and processes in this book will help with. In all of our relationships, including business, we need to know how to make the best choices for our lives, those that will benefit our desired experiences.

CHAPTER THIRTY FIVE

HOMOSEXUALITY

I'M SURE THIS WILL be the most controversial subject in this book. Before getting into the information about gay lifestyles, I want to address my opinion and point of view on homosexuality.

I'm sure many of you will think my statements about observations of homosexuality mean I believe it's something wrong and needs to be fixed. This is not at all what I'm trying to say. I don't personally have or believe in any type of bigotry or discrimination, based on sexual preferences. Personal preferences are unalienable rights for all human beings. In this matter, I'm very liberal. Although I have specific opinions on how things should be allowed, I believe in equal rights. Discrimination should be based on character and ability.

Stating I have discriminations based on anything may seem wrong, but as humans, we do judge. There's no way around this, nor should we try to find ways out of our judgments of life. It's impossible to do and only creates a false representation of whom and what we truly are.

If we don't judge character or quality, we can be limiting our life's potential and be put in unacceptable situations for who we want to be. I've been an employer. It's only logical that my judgments of employees are real and as truthful as possible, for the benefit of my life and any company who employs me. We live in a relative universe, where the idea of relativity itself is the whole purpose for having, needing and allowing for judgments. But what I am about to discuss is born from observations, not judgments, or just judgments.

When we look at people, we need to address character and ability relative to what purpose these individuals may serve in our lives. They may be friends, employees, employers, and mentors to our children, consultants and physicians in our lives. Judgment is about quality. When it's used to judge quality through character and ability, it can be done without bigotry or discrimination based in personal preferences.

My deepest belief is that life is an experience. The right to experience life in the manner, which makes me happiest, and to allow others the same freedoms, so long as this has no true, adverse affect on others is the highest human state we can achieve. Not only should we allow and accept those who wish a sexual orientation we may not like or understand, it's our responsibility to protect their rights to have such experiences.

I'm not fond of equality. There is no true equality in the universe. We occupy different physical places in the universe. At times these may be similar, but not equal. In making room for all, we should recognize differences. When allowing for equal rights, when appropriate, we need to interpret individual rights, when necessary, to protect those who may have preferences adverse to our own. A man is not equal to a woman. A gay relationship is not equal to a heterosexual relationship. Although many rights will be similar, each situation usually has its own unique traits, which should be considered. Blind justice, if truly blind, isn't fair. If we can't see the differences and special needs of individuals, we're missing a truth, as well as humanity.

Personally, I would never judge a person's character or ability based on their sexuality. I don't care about a person's sexuality, as long as it doesn't interfere with or become a necessary judgment point for the preferences of my life. I am heterosexual. A gay man pursuing me is not desired, nor would I want to offend a gay woman by pursing her, if I was attracted to her. Other than this type of issue, and aside from age and rape issues, people's sexual choices are theirs and not mine to judge. It's not my place to put legal hindrances in the way of their desired experience of life.

My observations of homosexuality have led me to conclude that, with one very small exception, this type of relationship limits possibility and are most often driven by fear and need for acceptance. I'm sure, after reading this chapter most homosexuals will disagree or will refer to themselves as the exception. We cannot all be exceptions.

You may be thinking the ideas I've presented for producing relationships we desire seem to be adverse to gay relationships. Some of them are, but not all of them. Except for the issues regarding the nature of gender, all these ideas can work for producing successful relationships of all types.

The gender issue is the reason I say this type of relationship limits possibilities. How is it possible for two people to have a relationship, two women, for example, when the female nature is to surrender to someone or something that will serve them, in order to satisfy their nature? How is it possible for two men to satisfy their natures, whose nature is to serve someone or something that will surrender to their services? It isn't.

The limitation in gay relationships is that only one person will be able to experience the true nature of their desires, at least at any given moment. The other person will have to use their intellect to play a role that's not the nature of their gender. No matter how good the relationship may be in every other respect, someone in a gay relationship is ignoring or hiding his or her gender specific desires.

While I observe homosexual relationships to have limiting possibility, I'm not saying that heterosexual relationships are doing much better in today's societies. I don't possess data to support such a claim, nor do I observe such a claim to be true.

I've observed that sexuality and/or sexual orientation are seldom based on the issue of what sex a person is. The preferences of sexuality are choices. By the mere definition of choice, which means an alternative, given more than one possible thing to choose from, you have and are making a choice. The choice may be desirable or undesirable, acceptable or unacceptable, but it's still a choice. I choose whom to love and have consensual sex with. I've observed the preferences of sexuality are based on acceptance, comfort, qualities and fears.

I would like to make it clear that I am defining the reasons why people are attracted to the same sex. Not that for some reason being attracted to the same sex is in some way wrong or needs to be fixed.

Let's take a look at physical and chemical attractions, which are usually the first traits experienced for sexual desires. We may think we're attracted to a given sex. Observation shows we're truly attracted to qualities. Do you find yourself attracted to genitals, hormones or chromosomes? Yes, the sight of female genitalia can arouse me, but that's more an animal instinct, connected to the idea of having sex than finding I'm attracted to female genitalia. I observe this as truth, through the thought reality that all naked females do not arouse me. As a profound lover of the feminine gender, it's possible I could find myself attracted to a she-male, if the person has some of the qualities I prefer and I'm not aware of the male part. I am proclaiming that if a person's sex is what I was attracted to than why am I not attracted to all who are of a given gender?

Ask any person to give you a description of what they may be physically and intellectually attracted to. Line up three or four people with these traits and let the person select the one they're most attracted to. Pull down the selected person's pants and reveal the participants aren't the preferred sex.

Many men can have all the qualities of beautiful women, except the genitals and chromosomes. The same is true for women. This is very true in today's society, with hormone therapy and all the medical and surgical procedures available to alter our appearances.

Again, we don't make choices for desired sexuality based on the sex of a person. Finding out that someone to whom we're attracted isn't the sex we desire can justifiably eliminate the attraction we felt. Still, their sex is only one of many possible determining factors in considering whether a person truly has all the qualities acceptable to us, which would motivate us to further pursue an attraction beyond any given point.

The choice of sexuality is based in quality and acceptance. Quality refers to the other person's characteristics and there are as many differing preferences as there are humans. One can analyze and debate what makes one person desire something different from another to the end of time, as the possible stimuli for defining personal preferences is infinite. There is no limit to the possible differences in quality choices.

We must learn to allow the differences to exist, rather than trying to define a level of acceptance for different qualities. I like vanilla. You like chocolate. Vanilla is my choice and chocolate is yours. There is no right or wrong choice, only a preferred choice, a different choice.

This means a quality, such as the quality of the opposite or same sex being a choice for an individual, can be observed as a true statement. We can observe the acceptance element of sexuality and see it has very little to do with the sex of a person. It has more to do with their looks, personality, character, common desires and willingness, as well as a truthful desire to be accepted for what we desire to be.

In other words, it's a desire to be loved for who we are, not for what others want us to be that motivates attraction. When who we are conflicts with where we are, we naturally look for, or desire, a more accepting environment. I observe that acceptance by others of whom and what we are is a large motivator in the choice of our sexuality. Although I have no evidence to prove this observation, I wish to suggest the question of its validity. I have, through my observations, concluded it to be the truth.

In long-term relationships, it's difficult and confusing if who you are isn't acceptable to the person you're with. I've observed all types of relationships, no matter what the differences of the persons and qualities are in different relationships, the issue of acceptance bears the same importance.

For outsiders who come into contact with a relationship with this issue, the strife can be unbearable and it's considerably more so for the persons in the relationship. When who and what we desire to be isn't accepted, supported or honored by other persons, life is miserable. It's obvious that, in these situations, we desire to look for a different situation and usually do. For the most part, nothing joyful comes from a relationship of this type.

Imagine a man with certain behavioral and/or personality traits that are defined as not normal. His quality is defined as below his existing community's respect and isn't acceptable to the majority of people. His traits are labeled and criticized negatively. As a result of this, he has various understandable desires. He may desire to hide, to stay out of the mainstream of society, possibly missing out on many of the wonderful possibilities in life. He may desire to act in a false manner, other than as who and what he desires to be, in order to fit in. He may find a group of people who are willing to be more accepting of who and what he wants to be, are easy to understand and observe, until he's able to find some place where he can exist to experience his life in acceptance of who he is.

We all want some qualification and assurance that our life has some value or worth. It's too bad we depend on other people's opinions of our worth and seldom find our way to provide self worth for our own existence.

If this man finds a group of people who accept him, perhaps praise him, for the traits of his desires, which others have scorned, it's easy to observe how he would choose to associate himself with this society, regardless of depth of quality or other terms of their character. This society accepts him for who he is.

Perhaps this society has certain behaviors they feel are part of their culture, such as homosexuality. Because the man has never had an opportunity to know different possibilities for his situation, he may truthfully feel he is a part of this. It's easy for a starving man to eat something he would find disgusting or refuse to taste in other circumstances. This analogy can be used for various situations, including women and business, but it shows humans can adapt for reasons that may not reflect what they desire or only desire.

Of course, we can be starving and still find something wonderful to eat. What I'm saying is that homosexuality may be a consequence of a situation or it can be a desired pleasure for certain persons, a desirable choice.

It's widely accepted most transvestites are not homosexuals. They want something that tends to be not socially normal. "Socially normal" is a label built by choice by society and isn't based on any relevant data or facts to determine its affect on happiness.

If society found it socially normal for men to have feminine qualities and accepted those qualities, without negative judgment or criticism, would so many men choose to be homosexual? If it were socially acceptable for women to be more masculine in their qualities, would so many women choose to be homosexual? If femininity in men was embraced and whatever masculinity women desired to portray was accepted in our culture, is it possible an individual who thought he or she was gay could find a person of the opposite sex who fits their desire and feel completely accepted for their choice? Is it possible these individuals wouldn't feel a gay lifestyle was the only place they could feel they truly belonged?

If society paid no more concern to the definition of how a given sex should be defined, beyond the fact that males have testicles and women have ovaries, would it have any affect on people's desired sexual orientation? If society practiced tolerance and embraced the idea of differences in mannerisms, desires and behaviors, would so many homosexual relationships exist?

I have little doubt lots of choices about sexual preference come from negative experiences, as I've observed this first hand. In these types of circumstances, professionals trained to understand psychological traumas are far better observers of the understandings of the truths for these situations. The idea returns to the observation of allowing the world to control your choices, rather than you making choices based on who you desire to be and how you desire to experience your existence.

Many injuries can truthfully keep us from certain experiences we desire. These injuries extend to the intellect, as well as the spiritual and emotional parts of life. Still, humans have found ways to overcome many injuries and go on to experience their desires. Every day, we see new advancements in possibilities for overcoming limiting injuries or conditions. Don't let your past experiences control your possibilities today. You can choose not to do so.

I've gone over a lot of issues regarding sexual orientation. The main reason for explaining some of my observations is to state that I observe convenience and acceptance may be more of a major influence for making a choice about sexual orientation than any other characteristic.

I've observed that convenience and laziness is one factor for choice of sexual preference. I've observed convenience and laziness is a motivator for many choices of human existence, not just sexual preference. Given the issues and difficulties in the field of peer pressure and acceptance in our societies, many individuals are motivated to make less effort in their choices for relationships.

If a group within society easily accepts me, why should I try to better myself in ways that require much more effort? It's easier to understand something with which you're familiar than to understand something that has characteristics with which you have no connection or knowledge.

It's much easier for me to understand the basic nature of another male than to understand a woman. However, there's greater attainment of knowledge and existence, if I make the effort to understand something different from me, like a woman. If I have a greater understanding of both women and men, as a result of my efforts, it will only benefit me in my understandings of the truths for my existence.

This allows me to make choices that better serve my desires, whether I'm attracted to the opposite sex or the same sex.

It's a great accomplishment of existence to overcome the gender gap. It allows us to facilitate joy, or greater joy, with examples of truth, helping my female partner to be what she desires to be and enjoy the experiences she desires in her existence. I can live knowing I have some worth and this worth is something no one can take away from me. If it is truth, truth is all that is real.

Yes, I've observed that sexual preference can come from convenience. I've also observed many homosexuals show very little ability to deal with their existence in other aspects of their lives. I'm not saying homosexuals are lazy. That would be moronic. I'm saying many choices made by inept individuals, including sexual preferences, are often based on the simplest, if not the easiest, existence. To be more accurate, the choices that seem to take less effort, at first, often produce a more difficult existence over time.

I don't observe that gay relationships produce a more desired experience than heterosexual relations. I've experienced and observed the possibilities are greater in heterosexual relationships.

Pleasure, or more pleasure, is one of the main issues I want to convey for most successful people. Some reasons for gay life styles have to do with the ease of obtaining intense pleasure, physical or emotional. But the ease of attainment isn't always the most advantageous way.

I surf, which can be very strenuous and both physically and mentally demanding. If I only surfed on warm, sunny, perfect wave days, I wouldn't be able to surf the best waves out there. I must surf on those cold, stormy, bad wave days, in order to be ready, educated and proficient in the sport of surfing and able to take on the best, the most demanding and the most rewarding waves.

Some would like to think that their desires and attractions have nothing to do with their life's experiences. In a general sense I see no observable truth to this understanding. Either way, how we become desirable of something will not change the fact that we are desirable of that thing. But understanding truths about our nature and how we come to be a specific way, whether these truths are elegant or just unadorned, will give us tools to achieve our desires.

If we are willing to accept that we have differing natures when it comes to the sexes we can use this understanding to make any sexual preference more satisfying. Two women in a gay relationship could use this understanding to work through and find some kind of solution to both their needs to surrender to a relationship, at least at some times, and find solutions to provide a place to get their nature fulfilled, instead of wondering aimlessly through relationships that never quite produce the desired experiences. Gay individuals who are uncomfortable with their achievements with the opposite sex can use the understanding of the reasons why they are attracted to the same sex to produce a more fulfilling experience with the opposite sex.

But a last comment on sexual preferences. Attraction, liking something, in this case another human being, no matter the reasons why we like something or are attracted to someone, we are attracted to them. And once we like something it takes great effort or trauma for us to dislike it. And I would easily agree that a bisexual person truly attracted to both sexes is living the highest level of existence for this subject. And it would seem arrogant and self-deprecating to try and convince someone who found all of humanity desirable that they were doing something abominable. You like something because you like it, no matter the reasoning why behind the attraction or desire. Please understand all I am trying to do is define the reasons so we can use the knowledge to live better existences. Even if the reasons I provide here appear negative, or offensive, to your desires, or even nature, and you wish to conclude some jdgment from me for what you think I think you are, which you would be incorrect about. I am looking for truths, no matter how the truths look, to use such truths for our advantage. I am over weight because I am lazy, not because I have some predetermined condition. I do not take offense from the accusation for the reason behind my state of being. Although predetermined conditions do exist, in most cases our experiences are formed from our environment and how we deal with our environment. If I want to experience a more attractive and healthier body I need to work at getting that for myself. If I find myself truly at distain with fifty percent of the world's population, like the opposite sex, I need to work at finding out why. Even if I could never be sexually attracted to the opposite sex, or same sex I should at least be able to love the ones of good charater and allow myself to enjoy everything else about them

CHAPTER THIRTY SIX

EMOTIONS

I HAVE NO MORE understanding of why emotions exist than I have of why existence exists. I only know both exist and emotions are part of the relative laws of our reality.

Nature is a least-of-necessity inventor. It produces only that which it must, in order to survive. It would be easy to say that if something exists, it must have some merit. With this understanding in mind, emotions exist and therefore must have merit.

Emotions, manifested by chemical reactions in the brain, which then produce specific feelings or behaviors, are not born of the intellect, although they can be influenced by it. I've observed emotions must come from somewhere else. Although we can suppress emotions and try to control them intellectually, through reasoning, emotions still retain influence over us, without our control over them.

The only understanding I can provide for this is that emotions must come from the soul, as a form of communication. Emotions are the tools that the soul uses to communicate its needs and desires to the physical part of our existence. These are powerful tools that influence the relative consciousness of individual beings that exist in this universe.

Wherever emotions come from, I've observed how often we deny, ignore and misunderstand them. Misunderstanding our emotions is yet another place for the confusion that hinders our abilities to achieve our desires. Once again, these are human, habitual behaviors we fall back on, trying to reason and use our intellect to tell our soul what's best for us. We've been taught not to cry. We've been told we can't possibly be hungry when we are, we cannot be cold, when we are. We've been told not to feel sorry for ourselves, yet we still feel so.

Almost all of these are untrue. Think about it. If you're young and impressionable and feel hungry and someone says you can't possibly be hungry, after all you've eaten, particularly if that someone is a parent, the most trusted person in your world, your mind must try to convince itself this feeling isn't hunger or that feeling hungry has no truth to it. Some of us have found the confidence to know and trust the truth about what we feel and we eventually stop trusting what we're told by others.

This is a very confusing situation for parents. We often don't understand why our children stop trusting us and rebel against the good advice we think we have and want to provide to them. I think it's obvious. When someone lies to me over and over again, I have no problem not trusting them, no matter who they are or what they do or what they mean to me. It doesn't matter how good their intentions may be or the high quality of their character. Once I find I can't trust that person's information, I stop trusting them and going to them for advice and/or information.

The mind is taught to not trust emotions, to find them of no worth and, therefore, not look for the truth behind emotions. The mind is a strong and powerful tool, capable of unlimited influence and abilities, which can easily override a desire. This is the danger of the intellect. Its power can compete with the power of our souls, by hiding and ignoring the soul's desires.

I've read in both spiritual and psychological texts that all emotions come from the mother emotion, love. I've observed this to be true. What we feel about something is due to having love connected to the subject in some way. I've observed that the emotions we feel are there to tell us something we need to know. We need to pay attention to that emotion, in order to please the soul. We need to adjust our course of action and behaviors, to achieve the experiences we desire.

If the soul requires health for the vessel and love from a connection, in order to experience happiness, then all emotion must tell us something about these two subjects. This idea is simple, deductive reasoning.

I'm leaving physical feelings of pain, hunger, temperature and such for a different discussion. I think it's safe to say most physicians can help us accurately determine our feelings about these physical emotions. We're able, as mature adults, to readjust the basic misguided truths for our soul's communications about the needs of the vessel it requires.

Let's look at some of the basic emotions, starting with the emotions of the soul, love and fear. Fear is born of the emotion of love, so let's begin with love and review my definitions of love.

Love is the adoration we have for someone we find unique, who finds us unique.

Un-acquired Love is the adoration we have for someone we find unique and wish found us unique.

These are not the definitions you'll find in dictionaries. The words they use for love include attraction, affection, desire, infatuation, sensuality and sex. But love is so much more than this. Love is more than just the love of a sexual partner.

Love is the adoration of uniqueness, as I define it above. You may not agree, but this definition even fits the love we have for children and parents. It may seem we have no control over the love we have for a child, but this love exists because these children are unique to us and we adore them for this uniqueness.

Fear is born from the idea of loss, especially the feeling of loss based on the belief we'll never experience life the way we feel it should be experienced. It doesn't matter whether this is because of the vessel's possible failure to survive or because true love may never be experienced. Are you afraid of dying? Why? Are you afraid of being alone? Why? Are you afraid of never being remembered? Why?

Because you're afraid of living a wasted, loveless life, which will end before you experience your desires.

Fear controls us all. It's a very real emotion of the unknown. Fear is what makes us want to look good. Fear is what causes us to forget love in the interest of survival. Fear can be taught, instinctive and conjured. Fear is what has allowed us to survive so long as the human race. It motivates us to create great machines of war, to protect ourselves. It motivates us to build walls, to protect ourselves from the emotional pain of life. Fear is what keeps us going, against all the forces that hinder us in finding a way to live the life of our dreams.

Fear is based in the issue of loss, whether it's a fear of losing our lives or losing our loves or losing our uniqueness, because of a soul's wasted existence. We build our fences, so no one can see how much we don't know, so we can look good and attract others, because we appear perfect, without flaws of ignorance or faults. From fear come all other negative emotions. Because of fear, we stop living authentically and start living the way others tell us we should.

To deny fear would be as wrong as to deny sadness or love. It's real. It exists with merit and purpose. Fear tells us to be aware of something, to carefully try to understand the situation we fear. Fear of the unknown is the greatest motivator of fear itself. However, once we become familiar with something and have an understanding of it, we often stop fearing it.

From these two emotions, fear and love, our minds, bodies and intellects produce feelings. These feelings can be defined as emotions, but they are created from the original emotions of the soul.

Joy is the feeling we are experiencing the wondrousness of life. It tells us what is real and truthful. Joy is an intellectual realization, in the mind, that the love the soul desires is being realized and is a wondrous and beautiful thing to experience. We love nature and enjoy a beautiful view of it. We love our children and enjoy seeing them laughing and happy. We love our lovers and enjoy making them moan in erotic ecstasy.

Excitement and all the other exuberant feelings you can find words for are derived from joy and simply define the level of the feeling you're experiencing.

Sadness is the overwhelming feeling that the body can't contain some loss to our existence and can be easily misunderstood. The biggest misunderstanding is that sadness is somehow wrong. That sadness shouldn't be experienced and should be suppressed. The belief that to be strong we must not cry and sadness should not be expressed.

Sadness doesn't go away, if it's not experienced. We only become sadder, when we feel we're wrong about being sad. If we want sadness to work for us, rather than causing us to react with impotence, we need to experience sadness when it's present.

Experiencing sadness in our lives, as though it's just another beautiful part of our existence, allows the moment of sadness to be expressed and satisfied. It allows us to move on from it. Sadness is an emotion designed for the soul to communicate something to our existence. Sadness is intellectual realization telling us something we desired to experience is, or has the possibility of being, something possibly gone from our existence. It can also tell us we're not going to experience, or we're not going after, what we desire to experience.

Embarrassment is a form of guilt, resulting from our intellectual confusion, when we don't understand the subject that's embarrassing us. This lack of understanding confuses us about how to deal with the situation. We react as though it's more important to not allow or desire such confusing conditions to exist around us. When we're embarrassed, this feeling is telling us we're either unable to understand and cope with the embarrassing situation or we know something is incorrect and have neither the ability nor character to respectfully correct the situation.

From our confusion and the fear others may find out we're confused, come negative feelings or emotion, including anger, annoyance, frustration and indifference. Negative emotions aren't always unproductive, although most are undesired experiences. They can be righteous reactions to unacceptable situations in our existence.

How can you tell the difference between productive negative emotions and destructive negative emotions? Hmmm... Did you read this book? You know the difference when you're experiencing negative emotions and you've checked everything you want to be on your list of who you are and what you desire to be. If you haven't been everything you desire to be, then the negative emotion is destructive to your happiness. If you have been everything you desire to be, then your negative emotion is telling you something or someone else is unacceptable in your existence.

This is a pretty simple process for eliminating most confusion from your life.

I'm sure you can find other emotions and feelings that exist. I'm not going to try to define every emotion, derived emotion or feeling that exists in human existence. It's enough to know what the basics of emotions are and how all other emotions derive from them.

If you eliminate confusion, not only will you be able to understand and deal productively with emotions of confusion, you'll eliminate them from your life and never have to address them again. They'll be absent from your mind and existence. This simplification of your life leaves you with much more peace of mind, by removing any need to think about and consider useless choices.

Humor isn't truly an emotion or feeling. It's a chosen intellectual response to a certain type of stimuli. The only definition for humor I've found that truly explains it is that humor is everything that's wrong.

Observe this and you'll find it a hundred percent correct. The laughter or disdain that comes from humor is the release of tension created by incorrect stimuli. Humor is simply that, something wrong.

Slapstick is someone falling down, getting hurt, breaking something. Jokes are based on mis-truths, sarcasm, irony and the like. Again, observe carefully and you'll find this is true. Understand, we can find joy in things that make us laugh, but joyful laughter is not humor. Joy is not humor.

We laugh at humor to relieve the uncomfortable tension that results from the confusion produced by a portrayal of something we understand isn't supposed to be taken as a real or respectful understanding of the topic.

Observe, also, the nature of humor makes it very simple for certain people to find certain topics not humorous. It's too difficult for them to accept untruths, which are disrespectful to certain topics, as something to laugh at. Again, our laughter at humor is the release of tension produced by the confusion or wrongness of the humor.

We all have the right to feel and be confused. We do not have the right to take our feelings and confusion out on other people. Others don't have the right to tell us we're wrong to be frustrated about confusing or difficult decisions or work, nor for being angry when we're treated unacceptably. No one has the right to tell us we should get past our sadness, when someone or something has hurt us.

Once you stop letting others be your reason for how you behave, you'll quickly see that most of the time their frustrations and problems really have nothing to do with how they feel about you. How they're behaving has no real affect on your life, unless you decide to allow it. You do not have to fix, be embarrassed by or feel disrespected, just because someone you've chosen to make important in your life is behaving poorly towards himself or herself or even you.

Try to understand why someone is behaving poorly, rather than reacting to his or her behavior. Someone who's not in a good mood is generally in need of support, even if that support is to give them time to get past an issue or time to deal with it themselves.

Love is water to the fire. Reacting to situations with the motivation to look good to others is the fuel for the fire. Support is using the fire to make a delicious meal.

Again, you have the power to make the choice. You have the power to produce your dreams. Don't think someone else's behavior is why you're not happy. It's possible, but highly improbable.

CHAPTER THIRTY SEVEN

FORGIVENESS

F ORGIVENESS IS A DIFFICULT subject. We all believe we know that to forgive is the best thing for us. I believe that leaving resentment behind and out of our lives is a good thing, but it's not always the best answer, if who or what we're forgiving doesn't believe they need forgiveness.

Sometimes, our dissatisfaction with a given person or situation is exactly what's needed to make a quality choice in our lives. I'm not going to debate the benefits of forgiving someone. I want to discuss forgiving ourselves for things we've done, things of which we're not proud.

When we're confused about choices we make for our existence, we have no way of knowing if our choices are the most beneficial for our desired experiences. "Knowing" when we should forgive ourselves becomes as much an issue as being "able" to forgive ourselves.

Confession, whether in church or just in our own minds and worlds, to those that deserve it or to ourselves, is the act of recognizing a fault or wrong choice, allowing us the possibility of getting past the fault or choice and becoming who we desire to be. Forgiveness only works to our benefit if we understand we're either in need of forgiveness or forgiving. You can't forgive someone who feels they don't need it. Trying to convince someone they need to be forgiven is usually a futile act. If you can't admit you may be wrong, you can't be forgiven or forgive yourself.

If your life isn't what you desire it to be, at least the spiritual or happiness part of your life, none of what I'm confessing to you will do any good, unless you admit to yourself – and the world, if necessary – that you've been living and choosing to live your life in the wrong way. In simple, plain phrasing, you need to be able to admit you're wrong.

This goes with taking responsibility for your own life. Who else is responsible for making your life work? Only you. The truth is, you must first admit that, if your life isn't what you desire it to be, you've made the wrong choices, choices not best for your desired existence. Starting with the understanding that what you've been taught so far isn't necessarily the truth is the only way to fix what you may desire to change. Forgive yourself. There's no reason to live in past regrets. Start making better choices for your life now.

"How do I know if I'm wrong or if I need to be forgiven and forgive myself?" you ask. Did you read this book? Go down your checklist of who and what you want to be. Are you being that which you desire? If not, it's most likely you need to state some type of confession, in the form of an apology most likely, for the fact you've not made the correct choices for who you desire to be. You need to try again. You need to forgive yourself for not making the correct choice in the first place.

Holding on to the guilt and confusion of a wrong choice is a waste of your time and energy. Recognizing your faults, failures and mistakes and knowing how to rebound, how to fix and move on to something more beneficial, is a success.

I've often been labeled as someone who doesn't think he makes mistakes, because I see no reason to hold on to them. I easily forgive myself, at least most of the time, when I figure out I need to make a better choice. I'd much rather be misunderstood as an arrogant know-it-all than hide myself behind behaviors to protect myself from others knowing I can't forgive myself for poor choices. I'd rather live without the guilt and confusion of holding onto shame for not being perfect. How my choices and when I change my choices look's to others is their responsibility to understand. The energy wasted on going over mistakes should be let go of, once we see and make a better choice for ourselves.

How and when to forgive someone else isn't as easy to discover. I usually see it when another person is able to see things from my point of view and understand why I feel they wronged me. Figuring out if something is unacceptable in my life, such as being wronged by another, is the same as figuring out if I'm being the person I desire to be.

I check my lists. If I've been everything I wanted to be, then I'm able to conclude that something is unacceptable in my life. Figuring out when and why it's time for forgiveness is beneficial in eliminating the confusion that comes with forgiveness issues. Once again, getting rid of one more place of confusion about my life provides peace, instead of discord, for my soul's desires.

CHAPTER THIRTY EIGHT

MENTAL ILLNESSES AND DISORDERS

J
UST AS I BELIEVE there are illnesses of the body, so do I believe there are illnesses of the mind and soul.

The body can become ill from bacteria, germs such as viruses, mutations and just bad conditioning, from poor diet and lack of physical exercise. I believe the same is true of the mind and soul. A mind can't work effectively, if there are diseases or bacteria or mutations interfering with it or if the intellect isn't in good shape from exercise.

Although such things don't directly affect the soul, it can respond to these things happening in the body and mind. The soul may become distraught, depressed or forlorn and either be unable or refuse to interact with the mind and body in a healthy manner. The soul may begin to send all kinds of uncontrollable communications, in the form of feelings and emotions, to the mind and body, as responses and consequences for not experiencing a more desired experience.

The soul can also become accustomed, as in the case of habitual behaviors, to having to behave in such uncontrollable ways, in order for it to feel as though it exists. The soul will pound on you, when it feels it's being ignored. The soul will also become sick and produce the most awful responses to feeling completely distraught, because it's confused about the existence it's experiencing, versus the experiences it desires to enjoy.

Doctors prescribe medicines for various issues and conditions of the body. Why, then, would we think these conditions have no affect on the mind or soul? Why would we think we can't have some sort of physical treatment to help or cure issues of the mind or soul?

Mental depression from emotionally draining events in our lives can leave us weakened. Just as a doctor gives you a painkiller to get through painful short-term issues of the body, he can do the same to help you through short-term painful issues of the mind and soul.

We take medicines for hormone imbalances and other chemically related issues of the body. Why not do the same for those who have chemical imbalances of the mind? Medical science has already determined most of our behaviors are motivated and/or influenced by emotions manifested from a chemical process in the body and mind. We live in a modern age, with helpful solutions for issues, created from our sciences. We should be able to use these creations to benefit our experiences, without feeling we're doing something abominable to our nature. We're a part of nature and all we do and create is a part of us being part of nature.

Medicine is good for the body, when it's needed. Correcting chemical imbalances, treating diseases, anesthetic and easing trauma pain are all good reasons to use modern medicines.

Our intellects have produced ways to ease our difficulties in life. To ignore our capabilities in providing cures, treatments and relief from ailments of our physical existence is ignorant and stupid.

Our physical existence extends to the functionality of our minds and intellects, as well as our emotions and moods. Science has proven chemicals and processes control all the functions of our physical existence, whether used functionally or recreationally. Just because we desire to be happy doesn't keep a chemical imbalance from depressing our body.

When chemical imbalances, diseases and short term mental or emotional depression occur, it makes sense to use the part of our existence, our intellect, to provide for our desires, to enjoy life, to provide relief from our suffering.

If I broke my leg, I'd have no problem taking a pain killer for short-term relief. Why, then, if I were suffering sadness or depression, even short term, would I not want to get some short-term relief from this type of pain? If I were suffering from diabetes, I'd take medicine to correct the imbalance. Why, then, not take something for a chemical imbalance that causes depression?

I'm not a doctor and I'm not suggesting anyone should take any medications or treatments without consulting a doctor. I'm just trying to explain that the use of medicines for one part of our issues is no different from using medications and treatments for another part of our needs. Medications and treatments all have benefits and possible side affects, but is useful for our existence and is just another part of our natural existence.

CHAPTER THIRTY NINE

THE AUTHENTIC LIFE

A UTHENTIC MEANS TO BE real or genuine. An authentic life is one that provides the truth for your existence, the truth about who you are, how you feel and who you want to be.

We're taught how to hide ourselves from this existence. Don't cry. Get over it. Be mature. Control your anger. You have no right to be frustrated. Do what you're supposed to do. Make me happy, make them happy, and be happy.

These words are powerful influences in our lives, but they're all about someone else's desire to look wise, through the guidance they provide and feel you must follow. The truth is, we feel what we feel. Unless someone asks us to explain what we're feeling, their guidance comes from a false understanding. No amount of commands to change our feelings is going to work. The only thing that will work is to experience the moment and see the truth for what's going on at that moment. We have the right to feel frustrated, there is such a thing as righteous anger and only I can make me happy by choosing to be happy.

The laws and rules for a good life have already been established. They were in place long before man walked this earth. No matter how we desire to change them no matter how hard we try to do so, to make them fit our fantasies, there's no possible way to change this aspect of our existence.

The only way to discover truth is for us to live an authentic life. Be sad, when we feel sad. Be joyful, when we experience joy. Observe what happens, when we're what we desire to be. Holding back and hiding behind our mental fences and walls will never produce experiences which allow us to find what is real and possible in this existence.

I was smart enough to realize I wasn't getting what I wanted out of life. I realized listening to the average person only produced more work and none of the results I desired. The only results from these efforts were more confusion. Now I am willing to seek information and the truth.

I finally had the information that made sense and the time and access to reevaluate what could really work, and a way to test the ideas I'd always believed were true. I found it's not what others want from me that produce's the power to have my desires met. It's the power I produce in me that results in the experiences I desire.

I stopped letting others define what should work and observed what actually worked. What works is being the light for ourselves. Make choices that produce what you want for yourself. You'll observe this is often the same as, or similar to, what others want for themselves. If you do this, the world and its people will see you as a light and an example. Your influence to produce your desires will increase.

CHAPTER FORTY

GOOD AND BAD

I DON'T PARTICULARLY LIKE the words good and bad, although I use them in everyday conversations. They represent very subjective definitions. What's good and what's bad is a notion created from our minds. It's not a thing, it's an idea. This idea doesn't remain consistent for measurability from one minute to the next.

Living life, based on what some source defines as being a good thing or a bad thing, is an impossible thing to achieve. The definition of what's good and bad is fluid. Once you achieve conformity to one source's definition of good and bad, you'll come across another definition with extenuating or conflicting definitions, which require further efforts of conformance.

There are over six billion people in this world and each one can provide you with a different set of standards for what's good or bad. Times change how good and bad are defined. I grew up with the idea of one type of diet being good for providing nutrition. Today, that diet's bad, because it's considered to have too many calories.

You can't hold good or bad in your hand. It's a mental and intellectual concept. Good or bad is what we decide it should be. Decide to be good to yourself, by deciding to be who you desire to be. Learn how to be good to and for yourself. Let the object of society's definitions of what is good for you and bad for you be the very last motivation for your behaviors and choices.

CHAPTER FORTY ONE

TIME AND PATIENCE

C HANGE IS SELDOM INSTANTANEOUS. If we want to change habits, it will take not only the work to recognize behaviors and behave differently. It will take time, as well. It takes time to learn anything and even more time to know something so well it becomes a habitual behavior.

Some of us have only a little more work to do, to achieve a specific goal. Others may have a lot of work to do, in order to achieve the same goal. If a mile is the furthest I've ever run, it will take time and patience to be able to run a marathon, no matter how well equipped and informed I may be about training techniques required to achieve my goal.

Changing your behaviors to ones that will serve you will help in the short term. Other issues, like self-esteem, will take time. Each choice you make, about how you allow things to affect you for the better, will be a tiny grain of sand added to your pile of self worth. Each time you stop yourself from allowing someone else to control the way you behave will be another grain of sand.

A few days or months of this may seem like little progress, compared to all the other piles of sand you've been building up over your lifetime. But after a year, you'll see this small, but substantial, pile of self worth. And it will be noticeable to not only you, but to everyone else. Once you see the self worth you've been accumulating, you'll know you are the light the world is trying to follow. The truth, for you, will be self-evident.

There is a sad point to achieving your dreams. Some people won't want to believe you. They won't accept that achieving understanding, peace, love and your dreams can be true for anyone. These people will mock, criticize and hate you, because they believe it's all a farce.

Stay the course for who you want to be, no matter what others say or do, no matter how they try to accuse you of being false. Not only is this the best thing for your happiness, it's the only way to deal with the situation in a manner that allows you to be an example for your truth and not provide support to those other points of view. The more we do, as we desire, the less they'll be able to achieve against us.

Never allow someone who is behaving nastily to you to be the reason for you being nasty in return. There's a time to stand up for yourself. Righteous anger is a real thing, but only if it's your choice, made from principles, and not a reaction to someone else's influences.

I'd never allow someone to hurt me, or the people I care about. I'd never allow someone to disturb or harm my life, just because they can do so and don't like me. However, each time I choose to understand, instead of react, I find myself much more peaceful, with less time and thought spent on self doubts about whether what I'm doing is right or wrong for myself.

Each time I add to my pile of self worth, I have a greater ability to be confident about the directions I've purposely chosen for my life. It takes time and being consistent. The person I am builds the rewards I desire for my life over the process of time.

When it comes to relationships, so many people have lived lives that don't support their desires that, when you show up to provide an example, the don't want to take the chance of opening themselves up to possible pain, in order to feel the pleasure which can come from trying something different.

This is the same for ourselves. We fear the pain we may experience, if we let ourselves believe in the possibility anyone can know about truth or the possibility of achieving the pleasures of our desires. This is only because our existence to date has been a continuous example that believing in our dreams only produces disappointment, at the least.

Now, you know better. You know the truths and are looking for truth in all things. You know you can have your dreams, if you're true to your principles and true to who you want to be.

Have patience with your efforts.

Time, at least what we experience and label as time, is part of our existence. We must learn that it is time that allows for proof of the truth.

AUTHOR'S NOTE

I'M NOT TRYING TO convince anyone of any belief, religious benefit or flaw in the discussions in this book. I am confidently observing that the understandings I've discussed in this book are a basis for living with any belief, or any subjects you desire in your life that you find important in your existence. So they can more confidently and constructively be experienced and can be a part of the joy in your life, not a part of your confusion.

I've tried to get my points across as quickly and easily as possible, without leaving out any information necessary to understand what I'm conveying. I'm assuming you have enough general intelligence to understand the simple and efficient explanations of the subjects and observations I've included. I am doing myself a service, by trying to create the world, which I desire to be a part of. I hope you find some peace in the observations of my existence.

I have provided a way for you to provide your own unique desires and definitions for who and what it is you want. If we find a way to eliminate the majority of issues we don't want in our lives, we'll no longer need to deal with them, because they won't exist.

Your experiences and desires may be very different than my experiences and desires. Your specific issues, needs and solutions will be different than mine. However, if we begin with the ability to understand the specific needs and issues of our unique existences, we can all find one of the many infinite solutions to issues we're here to experience.

I've tried to explain how we can define, for ourselves, the choices that best serve us. I want you to understand that confusion is the thing that keeps us from knowing how to make the best choices for our existence. If we can know the answers for our happiness, no one needs to explain it to us.

If you need a simpler definition for what human souls desire to experience, from my point of view, consider the following.

We desire to be loved enough to be remembered as something special in this world. We desire that everyone with whom we come in contact will have some type of attraction to us. We desire the information and knowledge we achieve and experience to be accurate to a truth, so when we share ourselves with others, we can be of truthful benefit to them. We desire to find some new, creative thing that allows immortality, more for the accomplishment than the recognition. Such an accomplishment can be as normal as a happy and successful family or as unique as being President of the United States of America.

All of these desires come down to the desire of love, the adoration for and from someone we find unique.

People are not generally malicious. For the most part, malicious behavior takes far too much energy to produce. Most of us aren't intelligent enough to be productively malicious, without others being aware of it and able to avoid us.

Most of us are just trying to be the best we can, even if it's unproductive. If you look at the world around you with this in mind, you'll tend to make better choices. Sure, there are people who have the time, energy, motive and desire to put forth the necessary effort to be malicious and/or purposely manipulative.

However, the long list of aspects necessary to be purposely coercive in our normal lives shows it's unlikely someone is behaving with intent to mislead for their benefit.

The percentage of people who are purposely coercive is very small. The odds are in our favor, once again, that it's a good bet, if you give people the benefit of the doubt, they're just as scared as you are and are doing the best they know how, in order to accomplish their efforts. That irritating co-worker you think is out to make your life miserable is just afraid someone will think them incompetent.

They are just behaving habitually, in a way that's worked for them for years, or at least they think has worked for them before.

Many of the people who seem to be irritants in your life are operating on habitual behaviors. Often, when they were young, they learned to be assertive, play shy, argue or fight for enough food to stop feeling hungry. They haven't found a way to stop behaving in a manner that no longer serves them. For your part, it's much more productive to be patient, to try and understand them – for them and you and your self-esteem – than to judge and accuse someone of being purposely coercive.

You may never be able to help someone else with their behaviors that don't serve them. You can, however, prevent their behaviors – which are really their problem – from affecting you. If you do this, you'll walk away at peace with the person who's frustrating you, because you're above the fear of having to make someone else wrong, so you can be right.

Many of the principles in this book are common understandings for most people. Some principles are, or seem to be, more important to some individuals than others. Different principles are important to different people. You may understand a point of view more truthfully or differently than I've explained it.

Whatever your experience or understanding of the principles in this book may be, before or after reading it, my gift to you is the knowledge of how these principles can be used for your benefit and how they all relate to each other, to work together to produce our desires.

The pursuits of knowledge, to help us better understand ourselves, and the reasons behind undesirable and/or uncontrollable behavior is producing a plethora of information. This information keeps us analyzing the reasons we behave and react to situations in ways that don't produce the results we desire.

Like the branches and leaves on a tree, the possible reasons for why we behave and react the way we do and the possible changes that can be made to try something different are immense, truly infinite. Believing we have the capacity to have control and expertise over such a vast amount of alternatives and possibilities is futile.

I've observed it's much more productive to narrow down the reasons for our behaviors and reactions that don't serve our desires. Reduce the list to key choices and spend your energy and intellect on producing behaviors that work, rather than wasting time on analyzing which parts of our behaviors have produced undesired results for our existence and why.

My observations have shown me a wide world of available tools and supplies to produce a more desired experience for our existences. We walk into our garage of information and find clichés ready for us to use to produce and create this wonderful vehicle of life we hope we can experience.

The problem is, we have no understanding of what type of vehicle to create and build, nor any understanding of how to use the tools and supplies to put any type of functional vehicle together. We're often loaded down with excess information, which can supply us with all that's necessary to produce any desired results, but we have no guide or training in how to put these supplies together, to produce a functional vehicle, much less a desired creation.

The human guide for creating and producing a desired life, from the tools and supplies we have available to us, is knowing how to make the choices we desire at a basic level. We must not let ourselves get lost in too many thoughts and possibilities, allowing confusion to stifle clarity for choice. Leaving your choices for how to behave and react to life to the basic influence of who you desire to be eliminates the need to even consider all the other reasons for behaving or reacting to life's stimuli.

WORKS CITED

Boteach, Shmuley. *Kosher Sex.* New York: Broadway Books, 2001

Covey, Stephen R.. *The 7 Habits of Highly Effective Families.* New York: Golden Books, 1998.

Covey, Stephen R.. *The 7 Habits of Highly Effective People.* New York: Free Press, 2004.

Holmes, Ernest. *The Science of Mind.* New York: G. P. Putnam's Sons, 1988.

The New International Webster's Pocket Dictionary of the English Language. Trident Press International, 2002

Scripture taken from the *New King James Version.* Copyright © 1979, 1980, 1982, by Thomas Nelson, Inc. Used by permission. All rights reserved.

Breinigsville, PA USA
19 October 2010
247589BV00002B/1/P